Anke Bernau was born in Germany but ~~~~~~~~~~~~~~~~~~ ~~~~~ e in the UK. She has taught at t~~~~~~~~~~~~~~~~~~~~~~~~~~~~~~~~~tly teaches medieval literature a~~~~~~~~~~~~~~~~~~~~~~~

'Bernau embraces wholehearte~~~~~~~~~~~~~ ~~~ing possibilities of her subject . . . [this] informative and serious survey spans the veiling of virgins to the death of dating . . . If Bernau draws any conclusion in her interesting and intelligent book, it's that virginity can never be fully penetrated' *Independent on Sunday*

'A timely and thorough book . . . sedulous research and polemical skill make for a fascinating, occasionally hilarious, and intermittently dispiriting study. *Virgins* is a book that reminds us just how fraught with public meaning our most intimate moments remain' *Telegraph* *The Broker*

'Virgins come in all shapes and forms. There are plump, pretty ones, like the Virgin herself, who look to heaven with a rapt, watery stare. There are mean ones, with shrivelled dugs and an abiding desire to get their revenge on a world which has let them down. There are martial virgin/viragoes, like Jeanne d'Arc, who manage to bend gender to their own ends. There are wise virgins, the kind who turn saving for a rainy day into an art and are probably investing in property even as we speak. And there are the foolish ones, who fritter everything away and end up morphing into the virgin's dark shadow, the voracious, incontinent prostitute. All these virgins, and many more besides, are up for discussion in Anke Bernau's neat little cultural study' *Guardian*

Chastity (a virgin and a unicorn), oil painting by a follower of
Timoteo Viti (1469–1523). The painting illustrates the popular legend
that only a virgin's purity could lure a unicorn out of hiding.

Virgins
A Cultural History

Anke Bernau

Granta Books
London

Granta Publications, 12 Addison Avenue, London W11 4QR

First published in Great Britain by Granta Books, 2007
This edition published by Granta Books, 2008

1 3 5 7 9 10 8 6 4 2

ISBN 978 1 84708 012 7

Typeset by M Rules
Printed in the UK by CPI Bookmarque, Croydon, CR0 4TD

For Silke

Contents

Acknowledgements

I would like to say thank you to the following people, all of whom have helped turn what was a daydream into reality:

To George Miller, for being a wonderful editor, as well as a fun one. His interest in the project made it easier to get through the less enjoyable moments.

To John Arnold, for bringing this project to George's attention.

To Wendy Knerr, for talks and information about sexual health issues.

To Sarah Salih, Liz Oakley-Brown, Clare Pilsworth, George J. Brooke, Rachel Rich, Anthony Bale and Luisa Cale, for inviting me to talk about my work, and giving me the opportunity to receive valuable suggestions and feedback.

To my colleagues at the University of Manchester, who make working there a stimulating experience. Special thanks to Anastasia Valassopoulos, Daniela Caselli, Eithne Quinn, Rachel Rich, Becky Munford and Naomi Baker for their interest, comments, support and wine.

To the students whose contributions have helped me think through many of the topics discussed here.

Virgins

To Gordon McMullan and Bernhard Klein, whose generous hospitality was the highlight of every trip to the British Library.

To Kathy Schiel, who made those trips possible by looking after Poppy and Jessie.

To Lena, Jackie, Tammy and Zoë, for not talking about virgins.

To my parents, York and Iris. To Silke and Jonathan.

To David, for everything.

Preface

Several years ago someone at a party said to me, without knowing what I was working on: 'You can tell everything about a person from their research topic.' He swiftly moved on when he found out what mine was, but the comment stayed with me. How did I end up working on virginity?

After I had completed my PhD on virginity in medieval religious literature I began to research virginity in film, and before I knew it I found myself reading up on contemporary virginity movements in the US. I taught courses on medieval women, on the body in medieval thought, on gender in early modern drama, and on contemporary women's poetry: sooner or later, all of these touched on virginity. And it wasn't just me: others, too, found virginity an absorbing and, ultimately, a puzzling topic. Mature students would talk about their teenage daughters, to whom virginity (and especially its loss) was still important, particularly in relation to how they made sense of their own sexuality, and to how they were judged by their peers. Others were surprised to find that they weren't quite able to define virginity: was it physical or was it an attitude? Those who thought it was clearly a physical identity would then struggle with the technicalities: for instance, does anal sex 'count'? The sheer range of responses was always surprising: amused, bemused, dismissive, defensive, embarrassed, curious, salacious. Never, however, indifferent.

The discussions that took place with students, friends or colleagues inevitably moved between the academic and the personal, the present and the past. The young nun in the Middle Ages, the eighteenth-century physician, the contemporary pop star, student or adolescent: each possesses their own understanding of virginity, as well as telling us something about the others. To paraphrase a fellow medievalist: while virginity is a question that has many different answers, it is nevertheless a question that keeps being asked in Western culture.[1] But there is more to it. For if virginity is a question, then it is one that has not only many answers, but generates further questions, many of which accompanied me while researching and writing this book. What is virginity? What identity can be described as virginal? Is it physical? Spiritual? Is male virginity different from female virginity? What does it mean to be a virgin? Why does it fascinate us? Is it still relevant? Can you lose it more than once?

When used as an epithet, the word 'virgin' conveys a sense of the unknown: virgin territory, virgin rock and virgin snow all refer to something that is pure, untouched, in its original state. Once the land is cultivated, the rock quarried, the snow trodden on, 'virginity' is lost. In a sense, this also describes the process of writing about virginity, for while much ink has been spilled on the topic, its meaning has never been fixed or 'found'. Thus, while virginal purity epitomizes order, it is also fundamentally unstable: it both assures and disrupts the status quo. This book does not claim to be a definitive account of virginity – it is more interested in looking at the questions, and then asking a couple more.

Chapter 1, 'I Don't Know Virgin', looks at how medical writings have defined virginity. Most people who think of virginity in physiological terms assume that it can be 'found' in the body; that the body can provide incontrovertible evidence of it, usually in the shape of an intact hymen. This belief – which is still widespread – is given credence by so-called 'virginity tests' that occur worldwide, in which doctors, midwives or other 'experts' are called upon to certify a girl's or woman's virginal status. In a different but arguably related procedure, women can now choose to 'revirginize' with the help of plastic surgery. Why are such procedures popular, and what are the consequences?

The second chapter, 'The World's Redemption', traces the most profound influence on ideas of virginity over the past eight hundred years: Christianity. Religious ideas about virginity remain central to how virginity is understood today, especially in its ongoing association with qualities such as purity or innocence. In contrast to medical writings, religious thought sees virginity as both physical and spiritual: what is important is one's state of mind. Today, virginity is making a comeback in the so-called virginity movements in the US. Located both at the beginning of human history, in Eden, and at its end, virginity is shown in religious writings to be always somewhere else, some time else: either in a prelapsarian, lost past, or in the apocalyptic promise of Judgement Day.

'An Unknown Alphabet' looks at how literary virginities offer varied but ambiguous pleasures, as audiences are invited to pursue them through generic and stylistic permutations.

Whether the agonies and ecstasies we thrill to are those of virgin martyrs, heroines of romances or troubled teenagers, virginity is shown to offer more than either physical intactness or spiritual purity. Here, a myriad virginities are conjured up, from the laughable to the desirable and the heroic. In the process, virginity and literature reveal their shared qualities: both are imagined, both are circulated, both are judged by the skill of their performances, both are either praised for authenticity or suspected of faking it.

'Repugnant to the Common Good', the fourth chapter, asks how virginity is related to the 'common good' of society, or the nation. Used figuratively to describe the ideal society, as well as to promote colonial ambitions, it provided a spiritualized and sexualized rhetoric of politics. How did this translate into the ways in which those same societies treated women? This question is explored in relation to rape law, arguing that the literal and figurative uses of virginity in society reinforce one another and, together, affect the lives of women in very real and often troubling ways.

The book concludes with 'The Future of Virginity', which outlines the fiercest debate involving virginity in the West today: that over sex education. The issues at the heart of this debate are: teenage sexuality, abortion, sexual health, contraception, sexual orientation and gender roles. Should teenagers be offered comprehensive sex education, or should they be told that abstinence until marriage is the only viable option? Both sides of this debate argue that what is at stake is nothing less than the future of Western society. The questions (and answers) of virginity continue to affect us – today and tomorrow.

Looking for the meanings of virginity leads to many places. On the way, we shall encounter love, truth, deception, death, everlasting life, violence, beauty, passion, disgust, heroism, passivity, constancy, fickleness. It is always about power: power to make meanings, the power to resist or transform them. Protean in nature, virginity's proliferation of meanings and desires ensures its ongoing presence in Western culture. Virginity is never lost.

1

'I Don't Know Virgin'

At the vaginal entrance is a membrane called the hymen.[1]

The elusive hymen

Although people hesitate initially when asked how one can tell whether a woman is a virgin or not, they usually end up remembering the hymen with a relieved smile. Yet the hymen is a more elusive membrane than is commonly assumed, and its status as sure sign of virginity is in fact doubtful. An article in the *Lancet* in 1978 stated that: 'Contrary to popular belief no definite criteria have ever been established for deciding whether a woman is a virgin or not', and that therefore 'it is extremely difficult for the medical examiner to state with certainty whether the woman is, or is not, a virgin'.[2] The authoritative tone of this statement demonstrates the persistence of the idea that female virginity is indeed physically verifiable, even visible and concrete. Female virginity becomes a universally accepted condition, one that need not be thought about further. This assumption is usually based on the hymen, whose presence or absence becomes central to a woman's sexual and social identity, as well as her self-understanding. Since determining whether or not a girl or woman still is a virgin (either to confirm her intactness for the purpose of family honour or marriage, or to discover whether rape or abuse has taken place) is a job that has often been left to medical practitioners, it is worth looking at the ways in which medical writings discuss virginity: how it is identified physiologically, and how it is connected to ideas about women's general health.[3]

A recent edition of *Mosby's Medical, Nursing, & Allied Health Dictionary* (1998) tells us that the hymen is 'a fold of mucous membrane, skin, and fibrous tissue at the introitus of the vagina', adding that it 'may be absent, small, thin and pliant, or rarely tough and dense'. Not only does the hymen come in a range of shapes and sizes – or, indeed, not at all – but even where it *is* present, it is not possible to use it as evidence for either lost or maintained virginity, for not every hymen 'ruptures' during intercourse and many rupture due to other activities, such as sports, masturbation with a vibrator, or sometimes even through the use of tampons. The title of the *Lancet* article already quoted is clear about the implications: 'The Doctor Cannot Always Tell: Medical Examination of the "Intact" Hymen'. Yet the hymen is still commonly thought to be the central sign of 'intact' virginity in Western culture today.

Female virginity has always been culturally important in Western society, but the hymen was not commonly discussed or referred to as such in medical literature until the sixteenth and seventeenth centuries, at which point its existence (or absence) was hotly debated.[4] Yet virginity was a physical state that was written about by medical writers and natural philosophers far earlier. In the high Middle Ages, when Europe experienced the so-called Twelfth-Century Renaissance, medical as well as literary, artistic and theological endeavours flourished, not least through the recovery, transmission and translation of classical and Arabic treatises.[5] Medieval scholars read and, in some

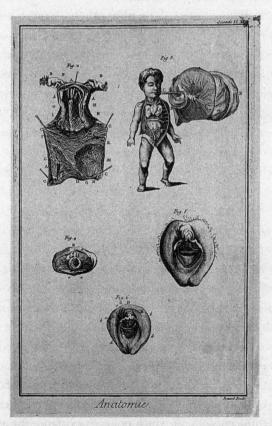

Late eighteenth-century engraving by Robert Bénard, entitled *The uterus, a foetus, the hymen and female genitals.*

cases, altered or added to the theories of Hippocrates (5th–4th century BC), Aristotle (4th century BC), Soranus (1st–2nd century AD) and Galen (2nd century AD), a body of work which was complex as well as, at times, contradictory. These authorities, especially Galen, Aristotle and Hippocrates, were to remain central to medical theory well into the seventeenth century.[6]

The gynaecological and obstetric works of the ancient writers did not refer to a hymen: Aristotle 'is silent on the existence of any "virginal membrane"', as is Galen. One critic has noted that those 'ancient and medieval medical and gynecological treatises' which do refer 'to an obstructing membrane or ridge of tissue treat such tissue as a medical problem. It is not a part of every woman's physiology, and it is not described as physical proof of virginity.' The only writer who does mention it, Soranus, does so in order to refute its existence.[7] Later writers in the Middle Ages sometimes refer to a certain skin – or *pellicula* – said to be found at the opening of the vagina, but only rarely mention a hymen. When they did, it was acknowledged to be one sign of virginity – but only one among many others, and not the most definitive.[8] The word 'hymen' is used by the fifteenth-century medical writer Michael Savonarola, whose description of it will seem very familiar to us: 'The cervix is covered by a subtle membrane called the *hymen*, which is broken at the time of deflowering, so that the blood flows.'[9] Its precise nature and even its existence were not universally agreed upon, however, even after the term became commonly known and used.

Uncertainty about this can be found not just by comparing the opinions of different authorities, but even within a work written by one and the same person. One seventeenth-century female writer, for instance, states confidently at one moment that the hymen as defined by the 'Arabians' does not exist, and in the next that the hymen is more loose and flexible in women who have menstruated for a longer time.[10] Another text from the same period unequivocally affirms the existence of a hymeneal membrane: 'For being whole [the hymen] is the only sure note of unstained virginity.'[11] This uncertainty continues. One eighteenth-century writer, discussing the case of a woman who wants to divorce her husband due to impotence, decries the requirement for the woman's virginity to be confirmed, amassing a wealth of legal, theological as well as medical sources to prove that there are no signs of virginity: 'The Inspection of a Virgin is both impertinent and scandalous: Impertinent, because it is presumed it can discover certain Signs of Virginity; whereas it has been nicely disputed and resolved of late Years in a great Assembly of Physicians and Philosophers of the University of Padua, that there are no such Signs.'[12] Jean Astruc (1684–1766), a famous professor of medicine who worked at Paris and Montpellier, insists in his work that while he is aware of those 'who have strenuously denied the existence of this membrane', he is siding with those whose 'judgment, and authority . . . have maintained the reality and universality of this membrane', whom he describes as 'all the more learned and able anatomists of the sixteenth, and seventeenth centuries'.[13] In the nineteenth-century legal treatise *Elements of Medical Jurisprudence*, the author notes that '[t]he physical signs of virginity have been the subject of keen discussion among anatomists and physiologists, and none of them has led to greater enquiry, than the *existence of the hymen*.'[14] Nonetheless, many thought that it was of great importance to be able to detect physical evidence of virginity;

one writer in the seventeenth century argues that nothing less than 'the repose of human Society' depends on it.[15]

Although it was recognized early on in the 'hymen debate' that the hymen could either rupture due to causes other than sex, or that not every woman had the same type of hymen, or that some hymens were more elastic than others and therefore remained in appearance 'imperforate', it has never ceased to be treated by many as a reliable sign of intact or lost virginity, by physicians as well as by non-experts. Even those writers who recognized the problems with ascertaining 'proof' of virginity often maintained that physical examinations should proceed: 'It is not to be denied, that many [signs of virginity] may be equivocal; but, notwithstanding, it is the duty of the medical examiner to notice them.'[16] The question of the hymen or other unquestionable physical proofs of virginity has remained contested until the present day. A scholarly article on genital injury written in 2004 states emphatically that all of the studies it examined 'confirmed the tenet that a doctor cannot determine from a vaginal examination whether a woman or a child is a virgin.'[17] Yet such tests are still being performed – often by medical practitioners – and are relied upon to determine a woman's virginity (or not) around the world, particularly before marriage or as part of AIDS-prevention schemes. The verdicts of these examinations can have serious – in some cases even fatal – consequences for the women concerned.

The signs of virginity

If virginity is not located in the intact hymen, where is it? A variety of answers were offered by works of medicine and natural philosophy. The late-thirteenth-century *Women's Secrets*, popular and influential well beyond its own period, suggests that apart from downward pointing breasts, other 'signs of chastity' are: '[S]hame, modesty, fear, a faultless gait and speech, casting eyes down before men and the acts of men.'[18] Urine also features prominently in such discussions: 'The urine of virgins is clear and lucid, sometimes white, sometimes sparkling.' A virgin urinates from 'higher up' than other women, because 'the vagina of a virgin is always closed, but a woman's is always open'. Certain plants, such as ground-up lilies, or 'the fruit of a lettuce' will make a virgin 'urinate immediately'.[19] Because the passageways of the female virgin's body were thought to be narrower and more constrictive than those of the woman who had been 'opened up' through sexual intercourse, it was claimed that you could tell a virgin from the heightened hissing noise produced when she urinated, presumably as a result of higher pressure caused by her closed vagina.[20]

Another sign of virginity, arguably the one considered most important (apart from the definitive negative of virginity, evidence of pregnancy), was blood. Bleeding as the result of penetration was understood as proof, not necessarily because of a ruptured hymen (although that was also suggested). It was thought that the tighter and therefore more sensitive virginal vagina would be injured on first intercourse, that the delicate blood vessels lining the vagina would be ruptured by the 'ineptitude of the male penis'.[21] This meant that pain – even 'extreme pain' – resulting from penetration was also a sign of virginity.[22] Or there was the proof of the uterus: that of a virgin was smaller, something which was said to be discernible by manual manipulation by a midwife. The virgin's uterus would also be less flexible, as it had not yet performed its function of opening and closing to admit male seed.[23] A more visible option is offered by Mrs Jane Sharp's popular *The Midwives Book* (1671), which advises that one investigate the shape and consistency of a woman's labia and pubic hair:

> [I]n those women that are married, they lie lower and smoother than in maids; when maids are ripe they are full of hair that grows upon them, but they are more curled in women than the hair of Maidens.[24]

One seventeenth-century writer lists all the signs traditionally thought to signal virginity, but adds that none of them is reliable: 'The Oracle of the God Pan, Insensibility of Fire; the bitter Water of the Hebrews; the Smoke of some Vegetables or Minerals; . . . [t]he measure of a Woman's Neck . . . [t]he hardness of the Breasts, the colour of the Teats, and the red Bashfulness caused in the Countenance of Virgins through Modesty' are 'too uncertain Tokens'.[25] A nineteenth-century expert takes a different approach in listing alleged signs of *lost* virginity: '[S]welling of the neck, rings around the eyes, the colour of the skin and urine'. He also mentions the popular story of a monk, who claimed he could tell a virgin by her smell.[26] Thus medical writers drew on a range of religious, legendary, popular and scientific sources in their troubled search for reliable signs of virginity.

Despite the considerable list of visible and palpable signs of virginity, all of these 'proofs' were felt to be inconclusive and therefore unsatisfactory. The suspicion that women might be faking virginity in some way, either intentionally or unintentionally, pervades many of these discussions and surely also contributed to their proliferation. In the late thirteenth century one text warns its readers that 'Some women are so clever, however, that they know how to resist detection by these signs';[27] in the eighteenth century not much has changed: 'the Signs of Virginity are far from being certain, because Women can easily imitate and counterfeit them, and so impose upon their Husbands'. The presence of recipes for faking virginity offered in some medical guides presumably contributed to a widespread and deep-seated anxiety: 'There are a thousand Ways of losing the Marks of Virginity, without having to do with a Man; there are, in like manner, a thousand Ways of recovering them again, when it has been really lost by having to do with a Man'.[28] A seventeenth-century writer sums the difficulties up dolefully: 'Women will contrive, and invent whatever may disguise the loss they have had, and it being impossible according to the words of a great King, to know the way of a Ship into the Sea, that of an Eagle in the Air, and that of a Serpent on a Rock, it will also be impossible to trace a Man's Enjoyment of a Woman.' He argues that, in fact, the only way of ensuring virginity would be to 'stitch up the secret Parts' of girls 'as soon as they are born', but adds that, because this idea 'is not in Vogue in France', education and prudence will have to do.[29] Yet others were concerned that the hymen, though ruptured, could grow back, thereby erasing signs of defloration.

What is perhaps the most striking aspect of the writings of many physicians, midwives and natural philosophers is that, as opposed to many of the theological commentators on virginity, they were not very enthusiastic about virginity. For them, virginity was associated far more frequently and consistently with ill health, even death.

Is virginity bad for you?

Although it was not the only medical or scientific model used in the Middle Ages, Galen's notion of the four humours was the one most drawn on to explain human physiology. Until the eighteenth century, the health of the human body was believed to depend on maintaining the balance of the humours: choler, phlegm, bile and blood. These humours were, in turn, linked to types of temperament (choleric, phlegmatic, melancholic, sanguine). Human biology was viewed as a microcosmic model of the larger cosmos: it was influenced by the planets and stars, and each type of humour and temperament was aligned with an element (fire, water, earth, air) that determined whether it was hot, cold, moist or dry.[30] Therefore the balance of the humours was thought to be susceptible to a wide range of outer influences, from the weather and the zodiac to the daily eating and sexual habits of the individual. This holistic approach stated that illness was a sign of being out of balance; a cure was achieved when harmony was restored. Regulation of one's nutrition, sleep, exercise and sexual activity was the focus of much medical advice. There was one main difference between the sexes, and this was caused by heat – or its absence. Since heat was seen as the sign of natural perfection, women's bodies, thought to be cooler and moister than men's, were said to be less perfect: weaker and more prone to physical and mental illness.[31] This lack of heat was also thought to make them more lecherous than men.

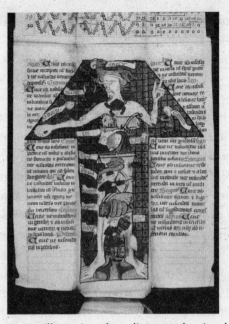

A fifteenth-century illustration of a zodiac man, showing the signs of the zodiac and the corresponding parts of the body they were thought to affect. This image was part of a physician's calendar.

In addition to the natural inferiority of women and the possible imbalance of humours, bodily processes such as digestion could also cause problems, particularly for virgins. While these processes were understood to provide the necessary and health-giving nutrients which the body needed in order to develop and maintain health, *excess* waste material would prove extremely harmful if not purged. Such waste materials included, for instance, 'seed', menstrual blood and faeces.

According to Hippocratic and Galenic works (though not Aristotelian), both men and women's bodies produced 'seed' that contributed towards the experience of sexual pleasure and reproduction. As a female virgin did not experience intercourse and orgasm, her unspilled 'seed' built up in her body, with harmful consequences. While this was also true in the case of constipation, the most problematic bodily waste product was thought to be menstrual blood. Whereas some writers saw the menses as beneficial to a woman's health – a monthly purgation that purified the body – others thought them toxic. As the thirteenth-century *Women's Secrets* gravely asserts, 'menstrual blood is extremely venomous'. The text goes on to say that 'a woman who has her menstrual period ought to hide her hair, because in this time her hair is venomous', explaining that 'hairs are made from vapors that have risen to the cerebrum, and these humors are undigested in women, and they are poisonous because of the cold that remains in them'. If you take the hair of a menstruating woman 'when the moon is in Scorpio or Aries, or when Venus is in Virgo' and place it 'under manure', the heat generated by manure and sun will cause it to rot. From this process 'a serpent is generated'.[32] Both popular and scholarly medical texts implied – or even stated outright – that a woman's body could be dangerous in its ability to 'produc[e] poison, in other words death or illness'.[33]

This 'natural' female toxicity is heightened in the virgin, whose closed body cannot successfully expel thick menstrual blood. Stories of the 'Venomous Virgin', whose stored-up poisons kill the first man to have sex with her, began to circulate at the end of the thirteenth century. Once the retained material had turned toxic the woman could pass on the poison to the man, harming him in the process. Perhaps this belief is also at the heart of the so-called 'Pest Maiden', who was believed to personify the plague that wreaked such devastation in the fourteenth century.[34]

In the sixteenth and seventeenth centuries, with the advent of a print culture and higher rates of literacy, medical works became more readily available. Translation from Latin into the European vernaculars ensured a wider audience for this kind of knowledge, which was often also popularized and made more accessible or titillating. At the same time a greater number of writers – some of them female – wrote handbooks on gynaecology and obstetrics for midwives and a lay audience. At this time, the medical profession was not yet the sole arbiter of how medicine was thought about or practised.[35] Yet while writers from the sixteenth century on may have offered different interpretations of certain illnesses due to newly available classical sources, and those in the seventeenth century placed a growing emphasis on empirical observation, they also still maintained many of the ideas current throughout the Middle Ages. Female physiology in general, and virginity in particular, were still held to be susceptible to a cluster of disorders linked either to menstruation or the uterus, most of which shared similar symptoms. This was not altered by Enlightenment thought, though there was a slow shift in emphasis from bodily to psychological causes for such diseases as hysteria.

Whether writers believed that an excess of blood was present in the woman due to the accelerated growth process of adolescence, or to the restrictive passages of a virginal body, or even to the absence of a pregnancy, they all agreed that it could harm the uterus if not expelled. In the seventeenth century, this was thought to result in uterine fits; in the eighteenth, women were diagnosed as suffering from 'vapors' and 'nerves'.[36] The centrality of the uterus, due also presumably to its role in reproduction, meant that it was crucially and intimately associated with a woman's state of health. On the whole, a woman's reproductive capacity was thought to determine her nature absolutely, while men were characterized mainly by reason. In this view, all women were to some extent hostages to their bodies, but women who did not enact or denied their 'nature' by remaining virgins, or by being abstinent for a long time, were bound to suffer graver and more punishing consequences. As one study concludes:

> Uterine suffocation (*suffocatione uteri*), uterine strangulation (*uteri strangulatu*), uterine fits (*furor uterinus*), hysterical passion (*passione hysterica*), green sickness (*chlorosis*), vapors, and many other terms were applied to the set of symptoms and associations that connoted a disordered womb.[37]

One of these disorders, suffocation of the womb, had a long medical pedigree. Sufferers of this disease were told that their wombs were roaming their bodies – a rather frightening and unpleasant experience, one imagines. The reason for this independent activity was a deficit of moisture, which in turn was due to the lack of sexual intercourse. The womb could also stay stationary, but in this case its resulting toxicity infected all surrounding organs.[38] Another variation of this uterine disorder is found in a text following Hippocratic theory, which outlines how a sexually mature girl who does not marry and experience sexual intercourse will not be able to expel the excess blood her body produces in its period of growth and development. As a result, the blood moves 'towards the womb ready to leave the body'. The mouth of the womb, however, is not open, and the blood is therefore forced back up and 'tends to become stuck around the area of the heart and diaphragm', pressing upon the heart and causing 'mental disturbance, including a sensation of being strangled, seeing ghosts and desiring death as a lover'.[39] This text became available in the sixteenth century, and exerted immense influence over gynaecological thought and practice. An early eighteenth-century compilation of medical and sexual advice collated from a range of sources, entitled *Aristotle's Compleat and Experience'd Midwife* explains the etymology of this disease in the following way:

> The Disease of the Womb is so called, not because the Womb is really suffocated, but because by its compression it endangereth the Woman's being so. For it is a Retraction of the Womb towards the Midriff and Stomach, which so presseth and crusheth up the same, that the instrumental case of Respiration, the Midriff, is suffocated; ... whereby the Body being refrigerated, and the Actions deprived, she falls to the Ground as one being dead.[40]

This violent contraction of the womb is caused by the usual suspects: 'retention of Seed, or in the suppressing of the Menstrues, which causes a repletion of corrupt Humours in the Womb; from whence proceeds a flatulent Refrigeration, causing a Convulsion of the Ligaments'.[41] The sixteenth-century French surgeon Ambrose Paré, along with many others, called this disorder *hysteria* and recommended that wives should engage in 'vigorous and frequent sex'; virgins should either marry or exercise.[42]

Chlorosis, a condition first described in the middle of the sixteenth century, is another disorder thought to affect virgins in particular.[43] It was said to be caused either by problems related to menstruation, sexual activity, or 'digestive factors',[44] and one of its more startling effects was to turn those afflicted a pale shade of green.[45] In many other ways its symptoms and effects were very similar to uterine fury, suffocation or strangulation, and it was recorded most frequently in the seventeenth and nineteenth centuries.[46] Whereas earlier writers had stated that menses or seed retained through abstinence could cause the uterus to move around the body, seventeenth-century writers such as Edward Jorden argued that the distressed uterus emitted 'uterine vapours', which affected the brain, thereby reiterating the Galenic belief in a connection between a woman's physical state and emotional state.[47] Once again, widows and virgins were particularly at risk.

In the eighteenth century the idea of the wandering womb was rejected, but the uterus was still held to be central to women's health, both physical and mental. Following on from earlier ideas on 'uterine vapours', medical writers from the seventeenth and eighteenth centuries onwards increasingly focused their attention on the connection believed to exist between a woman's mind and womb. 'Nerves' became central to explanations of women's diseases. Writing about the 'hysteric disease', Robert Whytt, an influential medical authority in the eighteenth century and at the forefront of this shift towards neurological models, states:

> It is true that in women, hysteric symptoms occur more fre-
> quently; . . . but this Circumstance . . . is only a consequence of
> the more delicate frame, sedentary life, and particular condi-
> tion of the womb in women[.][48]

The uterus and other conditions combine to cause a hysteric illness; however, he makes it clear that, in his view, the uterus is a secondary cause, for 'hysteric fits . . . often proceed from violent affections of the mind, or a disordered state of the stomach, as well as from a fault in the *uterus*'.[49] Whytt sees strong emotions as the prime cause of this female disorder: upset the balance of the 'nervous fluid' in the body and a concomitant disturbance of the mind ensues. In Whytt's model, body and mind reflect one another. For once, virgins are the beneficiaries, for Whytt states that they 'are often free from such complaints'. Perhaps underlying this statement is the old idea that virgins are more rational than other women – or are less exposed to the dangerous effects of excited passions. What is important is that this signals the shift in emphasis from physiological to psychological explanations for hysteria, even if the two were never completely separate. The final split between them occurred in the nineteenth century, at the end of which hysteria was no longer used to refer to the wide range of uterine diseases to which it had given a name for so many centuries.[50]

For most of the physicians and natural philosophers writing in the period from the twelfth to the twenty-first centuries, sex was positively health-giving for a range of reasons. Widening the virgin's narrow passageways allowed her to expel the liquid seed and humours that had been gathering in her body since adolescence. It also facilitated the flow of sluggish menstrual blood and even the expulsion of faeces. In addition, the sexual act as well as man's 'hot' semen were believed to warm up the woman's cooler body, thereby providing it with health-giving strength.[51] (This desire for heat was also used to explain women's insatiable sexual hunger.) The conclusion many came to, therefore, was that '[s]exual release was necessary for both sexes; sexual abstinence was unhealthy for both.'[52] Sex, however, could only be sanctioned within the framework of marriage, and so it isn't surprising to find medical writers recommending that parents should consider marrying off their daughter to a suitable man as soon as possible. If they did not, the clogged-up virgin was in danger of exhibiting a host of worrying symptoms, including physical violence, depression, self-harm and even death. But what was the *un*married virgin expected to do?

For those not able to marry, medical writers advised such 'relief' techniques as masturbation. Albertus Magnus writes in the thirteenth century:

> Certain girls around fourteen years old cannot be satisfied by intercourse. And then, if they do not have a man, they feel in their minds intercourse with a man and often imagine men's private parts, and often rub themselves strongly with their fingers or with other instruments until, the vessels having been relaxed through the heat of rubbing and coitus, the spermatic humour exits, with which the heat exits, and then their groins are rendered temperate and then become more chaste.[53]

It was, however, more usually suggested that girls should be helped by having a midwife rub them, or by having vaginal suppositories inserted.[54] Masturbation became a more equivocal topic for medical writers from the seventeenth century on, as is shown by references to women who, through excessive self-pleasuring or rubbing of their genitals, were thought to have greatly enlarged their clitorises to the point of making them appear hermaphroditic:

> [The] *Clitoris* in Greek . . . properly is called the womans yard [penis] . . . [S]ometimes it groweth to such a length that it hangeth without the cleft like a man's member, especially when it is fretted with the touch of cloths . . . And this part it is which those wicked women do abuse.[55]

Another writer adds that 'some lewd women have endeavoured to use it as men do theirs', but reassures her English audience that while '[I]n the *Indies*, and *Egypt* they are frequent, . . . I never heard of one in this Country.'[56] It was even thought (and feared) by some that the woman who remained virginal or abstinent could become highly masculinized, growing facial hair and blurring the boundary that separated male and female.[57] Therefore, although manual stimulation by a suitable person was still recommended to facilitate the expulsion of excess seed or menses in the sixteenth and seventeenth centuries, fears about female sexuality outside of penetrative heterosexual intercourse came to be expressed with increasing frequency and vehemence, a trend that gathered momentum throughout the eighteenth and nineteenth centuries.

Indeed, from the eighteenth century onwards there was a noticeable shift in medical writing, from a concern about illness arising from maintained virginity, to illness arising from an excess of sexual activity. Perhaps the clearest sign of the movement towards the de-sexualizing of women in medical writings is that while, until the end of the seventeenth century, the two-seed model implied that both men and women needed to experience orgasm (and, hence, sexual pleasure) in order to emit the seed needed for conception to occur, the eighteenth century saw a decisive shift towards the idea that women did not produce seed and therefore did not need to experience (and, indeed, did not want or were not capable of experiencing) pleasure through sex. This was further elaborated in the Victorian period, when physicians claimed that sex went against a woman's nature, and that only depraved or corrupted women could actively enjoy it.

This did not mean, however, that they thought lifelong virginity a viable option: women belonged in marriage and to childbearing – the latter was their ultimate purpose and sex a necessary but hopefully brief unpleasantness to be endured on the way.[58] Those who did not fulfil this 'natural' role were referred to as *viragints*, as living in an abnormal and regressive state of 'masculo-femininity' or even hermaphroditism. Among the prime candidates for such an unfortunate state were women who fought for suffrage.[59] The rise of a biological essentialism – which was used to argue that gender as well as other (such as racial) attributes were fixed, immutable, innate, biological and therefore 'natural' – provided the fertile ground in which physicians increasingly rooted their powerful interventions into women's lives. It was argued that by not fulfilling their natural biological destiny as childbearers, women were placing the 'future of the [white] race' in danger. As one writer fulminated in 1908:

> Nature is a relentless task-master ... We ... conclude that woman must degenerate structurally and functionally in proportion to her deviation from her fixed physiologic standard. When she invades the sphere of man in the modern business or political world, she departs from the sex-idea and becomes a sexless substitute for man. She destroys the physical and psy-

chic elements of womanhood without . . . She descends from a higher to a lower physiological level and soon shows the evidence of biologic retrogression.[60]

The women who chose to 'invade' the 'sphere of man' were associated with lifelong virginity insofar as, because they were *viragints*, it was firmly believed that no man would want to marry them. While chastity and modesty therefore became ever more idealized and mythologized throughout the eighteenth and, especially, the nineteenth centuries, *maintained* or actively *chosen* virginity was not. Instead, it was more likely to be associated with the 'new woman', who had perversely cast off her own nature and thereby imperilled her race's (and her nation's) shining tomorrow.

It might be an expression of this fear of 'impenetrable women' that the nineteenth century's main concern in relation to virginity and health was focused on the phenomenon of the 'imperforate hymen': the hymen that would not break and therefore would not allow menstrual blood, urine or faeces to exit the body, causing abdominal swelling and often intense pain or even death. It is somewhat ironic that practitioners at times referred to the imperforate hymen as the 'perfect hymen', even while describing it as a malformation and anomaly. In these cases, it was usual for the offending membrane to be lanced, which sometimes also resulted in the patient's death from clumsy incisions and ensuing peritonitis.

Between 1831 and 1919, thirty-three articles about cases of imperforate hymens were published in the *Lancet*. In 1832 one James Milman Coley describes the imperforate hymen in the following way:

The obstruction in the vagina, occasioned by a preternatural formation of the hymen, may be either complete or incomplete. In the former case the imperfection may remain undiscovered, until the menstrual secretion has accumulated within the cavities of the uterus and vagina, and has distended the former, so as to excite suspicion of the existence of pregnancy.[61]

The specific case he goes on to describe involves a sixteen-year-old girl, who appears to be pregnant. He treats her by 'push[ing] a double-edged scalpel through the hymen, which was very thick and tough', as a result of which '[n]early four pints of tar-like fluid gushed out'. She recovers, but begins to suffer from 'hysterical fits' from the moment that the retained menses pour out of her body. These subside only after she has 'menstruated profusely'. Once more it was young women in their late teens – those who were developing into sexual beings – who were most affected, even though very young girls and pregnant women could also suffer from this condition. More surprisingly, an imperforate hymen could also occur in prostitutes. The case study of the seventeen-year-old Elizabeth C., outlined in another article, tells us of a girl of 'lively disposition' who works in a brothel, eventually sleeping with a number of men, all of whom declare themselves 'unsatisfied' because they can not penetrate her. Despite this she contracts syphilis from one of her clients and, when examined, it is found that her 'hymen existed, and in a most perfect state and position'.[62] The question of whether or not she would be considered a virgin in medical terms is an interesting one, though not addressed in the article.

The supposedly paradoxical state that the body of a sexually active woman with an imperforate hymen represents is captured by yet another article: 'Dr. Wm. Hunter had the body of a young woman (brought for dissection) opened, and discovered a small foetus, although the signs of virginity were strongly marked.'[63] The author concludes that:

> The above cases bear interest in a medico-legal point of view, showing that sexual congress may be repeated, pregnancy ensue, and continue for the full period, without destruction of the [hymenal] membrane.

He reminds (or reassures?) his readers that these are infrequent occurrences. Yet even when lanced, it is reported that the hymen often grows back, becoming imperforate once more and resisting penetration.

What also recurs in the description of such cases is the combination of imperforate hymen, retained menses and the psychosomatic symptoms which were associated with hysteria, as the following article in the *Lancet* shows:

*** October 1843, 'Pent-Up Catamenia from Imperforate Hymen', by S. Swinnerton.

To the Editor – Sir: In The Lancet for the 16th ult. (page 876) there is a case of hysteria, &c., described by Mr. Rogers, of Bishop's Waltham, Hants. I had in my practice, about four years ago, a patient who was troubled with symptoms resembling those of Ann Burgess, as detailed by Mr. Rogers – dragging of the leg and dyspnoea [breathing difficulties].

A sense of weight and fullness in the hypogastric region led to the examination of the hymen, which I found much distended, pressed outward, and imperforate. On dividing that membrane, more than two quarts of collected menstruous fluid escaped, of the consistency of treacle; after which all the urgent symptoms quickly abated, with the exception of dragging the leg. That continued, but gradually improved in four or five months, when the patient got quite well, and has continued well to the present time, menstruating regularly.[64]

The old idea of 'opening up' the virgin in order to restore her health and, presumably, to ensure her successful circulation on the marital and reproductive circuit, is still recognizable here.

Yet even the woman who *did* lose her virginity came to be seen as a threat, whether or not this occurred within the 'proper' marital bounds. In his article on 'The Taboo of Virginity' (1918), Sigmund Freud describes virginity as a state notable not primarily for its physical characteristics, but for the psychological turmoil that ensues when a woman 'loses' it. He argues that at the point of first penetrative intercourse the woman experiences 'hostile bitterness against the man', due to her penis envy, 'which never completely disappears in the relations between the sexes, and which is clearly indicated in the strivings and in the literary productions of "emancipated" women'.[65]

The man who takes upon himself a woman's 'immature sexuality' thus exposes himself to danger, for 'the motives which seek to drive a woman to take vengeance for her defloration are not completely extinguished even in the mental life of the civilised woman'.[66] It is noticeable that while Freud ascribes penis envy to all women, he emphasizes the particular case of the '"emancipated" woman'. Virginity, it seems, is always potentially dangerous to someone's health.

Restoring virginity and the chastity business

A separation of physical and psychological virginity is difficult to make. Although contemporary commentators may scoff at the notion that virginity remains important in a secular, sexually liberal West, there is considerable evidence to show that it is still central to how women, in particular, view themselves and are viewed by others, both physically *and* psychologically. It is important to consider, for instance, why those whose only experience of sex is violent or abusive often seek reassurance that they are still virgins. In cases where the abuse has caused genital injury, surgery is performed in order to achieve 'a more normal postoperative appearance of the vagina and hymen'.[67] Part of this procedure must surely be to aid the woman (or child) in her emotional and psychological recovery, as much as for physiological reasons.

It is often argued that Western thinking about sexuality changed fundamentally in the 1960s and 1970s, as a result of 'feminist, youth counterculture, and gay rights movements'.[68] While this is undoubtedly true, some older views have persisted, even if they are couched in different terms. In this same period, the focus of the discussion on virginity moved from the medical realm overtly into the realm of sociology: medical textbooks today do not waste much ink on virginity. Virginity itself is no longer linked to particular illnesses, even while there still are 'female illnesses' today, such as PMS (premenstrual syndrome), whose symptoms uncannily echo those of uterine suffocation, chlorosis or vapours.[69]

Although virginity itself is no longer part of these associations, this does not mean that it has become unimportant, or that medicine does not still participate in the perpetuation of virginity's many myths.

A striking and troubling contemporary example of this is the phenomenon of cosmetic vaginal surgery.[70] While in the mid-twentieth century women were more likely to ask gynaecologists to perform a procedure known 'hymenotopy' – the cutting of the hymen – in order to experience less discomfort on their wedding nights,[71] the trend today seems to be going in the opposite direction.

The ever-increasing number of clinics offering 'hymen restoration' attests to the persistence of a virginal ideal in Western culture. Here virginity is advertised as a commodity that can be acquired at any time – as long as one can pay. The clinics in question promise to 'repair *or augment* the hymen to restore it to its "virginal" state'.[72] This procedure is referred to as hymenoplasty or hymenorraphy, hymenal reconstruction or as 'hymen repair surgery'. The glossy promotion material acknowledges the potential failure of the hymen to 'deliver' in its promise to enhance what has, in some cases, never been 'lost' in the first place. While this surgery does cater for women who have lost their virginity and want to 'regain' it (for whatever reason), the service is also used by women who have *never* had sex but fear that their hymen might not be intact enough: 'Using a special surgical technique we can repair and tighten the hymen to a *more intact, virgin-like state*'. Because this surgery is 'customize[d] . . . to the individual needs and expectations of the patient', it is (in 'most cases') '*virtually undetectable*'.[73]

Those involved in performing hymen repair procedures

market themselves as trained professionals and trade on the language of medical expertise, with its objectivity and authority, sometimes underlined by a website banner proclaiming: 'Board Certified Plastic Surgeon'. Yet there is no known physiological function that the hymen fulfils, so despite the terminology and qualifications used to reassure the client of the professional and 'medical' nature of the procedure, it is undeniably purely in the service of either supporting or creating certain cultural demands – and not just those of barbaric, 'other' cultures out there, as it is sometimes suggested.[74]

Some of the websites almost acknowledge this, although they rather disingenuously conflate 'personal' and 'cultural': 'Sometimes, for cultural or *other personal* reasons ... a woman would like to restore a more intact, tighter hymenal ring.'[75] It is often claimed that such procedures protect women who come from cultures where unfulfilled proof of virginity can lead to a woman's death. They also, however, reinforce and perpetuate the very myth of provable virginity that endangers these women in the first place. Any objection to hymenoplasty is swatted away as a sign of intolerance for and ignorance of other cultures: instead, hymeoplasty is promoted as a service that the benign West offers to help women of benighted, backward cultures.[76]

Indeed, one such site has a specific disclaimer added to its information on hymenoplasty, differentiating it from other cultural practices which might seem uncomfortably similar: '[T]his surgery is done for the *personal* benefit of the *individual* patient. We absolutely do not provide or condone any form of female circumcision or genital mutilation, regardless of one's cultural beliefs.' This is fascinating: hymenoplasty is a purely personal choice, while female circumcision is a cultural belief. Hymenoplasty and other procedures such as 'vaginal rejuvenation' are 'enhancement', while female circumcision is 'mutilation'. The implication is that the concept of 'individual choice' – representative of Western ideals – is somehow not cultural, as if Western women exist in a vacuum where they are entirely free agents. *Other* cultures demand unreasonably that women be virgins on their wedding night; *we* just happen to like the idea for entirely personal reasons. It is true that Western women today would not expect to be violently punished for being sexually active before marriage; however, while hymenal reconstruction does not bring with it the health dangers associated with female genital mutilation, it would be naive – even mendacious – to suggest that by choosing to submit to hymenoplasty or other cosmetic vaginal surgery women are not at all influenced by their own culture's frequently coercive ideals of female beauty and desirability.[77]

At the centre of this practice – regardless of the spin – lie ideas linked intimately to the idealization of virginity and the myriad qualities it still represents: youth, inexperience, purity, tightness. Some Western surgeons and clinics might want to dress it up as an individualist, capitalist-consumer 'choice', but ultimately it is only desirable because Western culture – like many others – still fetishizes virginity and youthfulness. This is in fact confirmed by the whole panoply of surgical procedures that are offered to women with the aim of remodelling their vaginas: as well as 'vaginal rejuvenation', women can have 'labia reduction', 'clitoral hood removal', 'labia majora augmentation', 'vagina reduction', 'mons pubis liposuction' and more, in order to achieve the elusive and tyrannical body beautiful – and to keep their partners or husbands sexually satisfied.[78] It is worth noting that most of these procedures are aimed at making the vagina look and feel plumper, neater and tighter – in other words, to make it look more like that of a young girl. Of a virgin, in fact, when virginity is associated primarily with the fantasy of adolescent nubile innocence.

In these contemporary promotions of physical virginity the implication is that virginity is actually beneficial to the woman's psychological and physical well-being, a departure from much of the earlier material. The message here is that a Western woman who chooses hymenoplasty is exercising her personal choice and asserting control over her body in a positive way, thereby both expressing and bolstering her sense of self. Choosing 'virginity' in this way is therefore pro-active: a sign of knowing what you want and getting it.

Virgin mummies

While there have always been some medical commentators (though usually a minority) who argue that maintained virginity could be good for you, there have been times and places when *someone else's* virginity has been recommended as curative. From the twelfth century on, due to a mistranslation by Gerard of Cremona of a medical text written by the 9th–10th-century Persian physician al-Razi (Rhazes), what had been described in the Arabic as the particularly health-giving bitumen ('*mumiya*') became, in the Latin, the particularly health-giving bodily fluid of corpses found in Egyptian tombs ('*mumia*'): 'Mumia, this is the mumia of the sepulchers with aloes and myrrh mixed with the liquid (*humiditate*) of the human body.'[79] It was mistakenly thought that the corpses (which became known as 'mummies') were the source of this panacea, which was immensely popular throughout Europe until the sixteenth and seventeenth centuries, to such an extent that a vigorous trade in cadavers of criminals and the poor, sold as genuine ancient 'mummies', came into existence to meet demand. Virginal *mumia* was considered to be the most beneficial and was therefore also the most expensive.[80] It is not recorded how one could tell whether a particular mummy was a virgin or not.

2

'The World's Redemption'

Maidenhood is the treasure that once lost can never be found.[1]

Body and soul

In Christian thought, being – and remaining – a true virgin is not easy or straightforward. In fact, it is one of the hardest things to achieve. Although we tend to look to medicine for definitions of virginity, religion was the supreme authority for most of the past eight hundred years. The centrality of religious institutions and learning in Western culture over the centuries has meant that they shaped the way virginity was understood in the wider culture as well. Even though we might not always be aware of it, this influence is still evident today. Medieval Catholicism, drawing on the writings of Church Fathers such as Jerome and Ambrose, saw virginity as the most exalted of all states of being, especially for women. While the Reformation and Protestantism changed and diversified the ways virginity was understood within Western culture, its importance remained. Far beyond the Middle

Ages, it was referred to by religious writers – Catholic and Protestant – as a priceless, unique treasure, easily lost and never regained.

Nicolas Venette, writing in the seventeenth century, claims that the difference between a religious and a medical under-standing of virginity is that, for the former, virginity is a 'Virtue of the Soul, that has nothing common with the Body', while, for the latter, it is merely 'a choice Collection of the secret Parts of a Woman, that has not been spoiled by the approach of a Man.'[2] It is certainly true that for religious thinkers, virginity is not *primarily* a physical state. Although physical integrity is central to being a virgin, the thirteenth-century treatise on virginity *Holy Maidenhood* reminds its audience that this on its own is not enough: '[T]hough you, maiden, are still whole in body, if you have pride, envy or anger, avarice or weak will deep in your heart, you prostitute yourself with the devil from hell'.[3] Nonetheless, the impor-tance of physical virginity cannot be denied. If a maiden is not careful, lechery 'strikes the power of maidenhood and wounds her gravely'. Should she agree to the 'sorry act at the end' – presumably sexual intercourse – her maidenhood will receive a 'deathblow', from which it 'never revives'.[4] The flesh is the enemy which needs to be tamed, 'with fasting, with keeping vigil, with haircloth, with hard work, with harsh disciplines'.[5] Loss of virginity begins in the soul and is finalized in the body.

Spiritual and physical virginity therefore both require con-stant vigilance and protection; but while one cannot be a true virgin without spiritual purity, it is even harder to claim vir-ginity without physical intactness. Early medieval narratives and historical documents contain exemplary accounts of reli-gious women who mutilate themselves rather than risk being raped in times of war and invasion. Cutting off their noses or upper lips, they hope that their disfigurement will protect them; as a result, their frustrated attackers often kill them in revenge. Though there were writers who argued that virgins who were raped remained virginal, suspicion about the woman's complicity in the act – or inadvertent enjoyment of it due to her essentially lascivious nature – always remained.

Virginity was valued in both secular and religious spheres of life throughout the Middle Ages and beyond, but it didn't mean the same thing for both. The virginity of a young girl destined to become the wife of an aristocrat, for instance, was considered necessary primarily in order to guarantee the legitimacy of offspring and, thereby, the untroubled transfer of property and title from one generation to the next.[6] For those who chose to follow a religious vocation, however, the purity virginity represented became increasingly central to the way in which a religious identity was understood and how it was displayed to the outside world. From the Gregorian Reform of the Church (mid-eleventh century) onwards, priests as well as monks and nuns were exhorted to remain celibate (ideally virginal) and to understand this as a main marker of their difference from those living secular lives. The reasons given for the necessity of a celibate clergy were part of an aggressive attack on what were thought to be the sources of defilement threatening the integrity of a pure clergy, and reducing its authority.[7] Celibacy and virginity, it was thought, would help to shore up the clergy's claim of moral and spiritual superiority.

The most frequent cause of this kind of contamination was said to be the presence of women, since women's 'sexual presence polluted the minister of the altar'. Women were also seen, rather less spiritually, as 'a drain on church resources'.[8] The demand for clerical celibacy made as part of the Gregorian Reform caused considerable tensions within the Church as many priests were married, and there was always resistance in some quarters to this idea. What happened to the women who were priests' wives in this period is largely unknown, but one can imagine that destitution and prostitution were frequently their lot. The drive for clerical purity also had a far-reaching and lasting effect on how women were perceived in the wider culture, consolidating the view that they were creatures ruled by the demands of the flesh, rather than those of the spirit. The Gregorian Reform succeeded both in 'mak[ing] the ordinary woman suspect' and in promoting 'the Virgin Mary . . . as her purified substitute'.[9] The polar opposition of virgin and carnal woman, in which each and every woman is always already a member of the latter category simply by virtue of *being* a woman, was here confirmed and strengthened once more.

It does not come as a surprise, then, that virginity was believed to 'improve' women. As we have seen, medical theories at this time stated that women were physically inferior to men. Religious writers added that women were spiritually inferior. Men were guided by the spirit, women by the flesh. Being male was considered desirable, and women were believed to become more 'masculine' (and therefore more perfect) if they turned away from their carnal natures. Virginity was the surest way of achieving this, for virginity was understood as a triumph over physicality and worldly sinfulness. As St Jerome said, the woman who dedicates herself to Christ rather than to the world 'ceases to be a woman (*mulier*) and is called a man (*vir*)', since 'we all aspire to the condition of

A fifteenth-century miniature of St Ursula and the Eleven Thousand Virgins. The British virgin Ursula and her host of fellow virgins achieved martyrdom in Cologne in the year 452 AD, when they were murdered by the Huns besieging that city.

perfect manhood'.[10] One type of narrative that celebrates this masculinization is that of the transvestite virgin, popular from the second century to the sixteenth. In these stories, a young girl, reaching marriageable age, disguises herself as a monk in order to escape marriage (and, in some cases, a pagan community) and to preserve her virginity for Christ. Usually she joins a male monastic community, living there until her death results in her female identity being made known, to the wonder of all. In this disguise, the virgins sometimes achieve positions of real power. Eugenia, for instance, who enters a monastery to serve Christ, is so successful in her male role that her fellow monks eventually elect her as their abbot. She is even accused of seduction by a widow who was smitten with the young 'monk's' good looks and gentle manner. In other saints' legends, virgins pray for physical disfigurements or a fatal illness so that their prospective bridegrooms will reject them, and free them from unwanted marriage. In the life of St Wilgefortis, for instance, this masculinization of the virgin saint is represented by the beard that grows on her face when she prays for help, which has the desired effect of considerably lessening her charms for her suitor.

While it would be possible to argue that virginity constituted a kind of 'third' gender, the ways in which it was discussed and promoted by theologians challenge this assumption. Although virginity was recommended for both men and women following a religious life, it was emphasized far more in the literature aimed at women. In the stories of the transvestite saints, for instance, it is notable that cross-dressing always works in one direction: from female to male. Striving to be more like a man was understood as a self-evident desire for self-improvement on the part of the virgins who undertook it; the opposite could never happen, since that would entail a diminishing of status, a step down in the God-given order of things.[11]

The anxiety that one often finds in writings on virginity is rooted in both misanthropic and misogynist views. Human beings were fallen creatures, and women in particular were not to be trusted. Stories of feigned virginity appear wherever the culture places a great value on purity and reveal a fear that there is no secure way of policing this elusive state of being. Considering these different aspects of a religious understanding of virginity, it is not surprising that the *loss* of virginity by someone dedicated to a religious life could never just be viewed as a personal choice or experience. Anxiety about the authenticity of someone's virginity was omnipresent (how could one know for sure?), and religious writers urged those living a religious life to be constantly vigilant so that they would not endanger their purity through careless behaviour or unguarded thoughts. While the dire consequences of losing one's virginity were vividly outlined in terms of individual loss, conjuring up images of shame and painful damnation, the loss of a religious person's virginity also had wider consequences, throwing doubt on the purity in the community to which she belonged, and weakening the Church's authority.

The tragic events of the life of the anonymous Nun of Watton are related in a twelfth-century manuscript by Aelred, abbot of the Cistercian monastery of Rievaulx, the ruins of which can still be visited in Yorkshire. The abbot describes the scandalous event that occurred in the Gilbertine nunnery of Watton in Yorkshire: a girl was given at the age of four to the convent as an oblate, an offering of devotion. Aelred tells us that she grew into a flighty young girl, who does not take to the religious life. Since the Gilbertines were an order that allowed double houses – houses that included both monks and nuns – the young nun eventually meets a young brother, with whom she flirts and arranges secret meetings. When Aelred relates how she goes to her first tryst, he concludes, horrified: 'Block your ears, virgins of Christ, and close your eyes. She walks out the virgin of Christ; shortly after she returns an adulteress.'[12] When she is found by the other nuns to be pregnant, their anger is terrible: 'Their zeal burned in their bones, and . . . [s]ome believed that she should be tied to a tree and roasted over charcoal'. Restrained by the older nuns, the younger ones finally agree not to kill her; instead, they strip her, whip her, bind her in chains and lock her in a bare cell, where she is fed nothing but bread and water. When she confesses to them that she had arranged to run away with her lover, they capture the brother and bring him to his pregnant paramour, who is forced to castrate him. His severed genitals are shoved into her mouth, 'foul and bloody and just as they were'. In Aelred's view, the nuns are 'avengers of uncleanness', whose harsh punishment of the girl and her lover 'avenges the injury to Christ'.[13]

This story shows how the loss of the individual nun's virginity is understood by the other nuns – as well as by Aelred himself – as a communal affront and crime. And this is an accurate perception, since the Gilbertines had to defend their double houses against repeated accusations and suspicions of sexual impropriety. As one critic notes, 'whether a cause or a symptom, the affair at Watton marks the beginning of the period when the sexes were again segregated' in religious communities.[14] What we see in this act of raging retribution is a fear for the community itself: the individual nun's breached and now impure body could come to stand as a symbol for the entry of sin into the community: after all, if *she* couldn't maintain her virginity, who's to say that the others can or do? In a culture in which the claim of purity is always viewed with suspicion and doubt, such a scandal threatens that one can never be vigilant enough.

In addition to being both physical and spiritual, virginity is imbued with a range of potent symbolic meanings that signify the relationship between Christ and the Church, and between the Church and the believer. Catholic thinkers pointed out that the two main figures of worship in Christianity – Christ and the Blessed Virgin Mary – were virgins, and they were extolled as ideals which believers should aspire to. And while some men or women might decide to live chastely, or to abstain from sex, this is not the same as virginity. As one twentieth-century Catholic writer explains:

> If virginity and celibacy be distinguished as two forms of the state of abstinence consecrated to God, virginity is then to be understood in the sense of intact abstinence, while celibacy does not necessarily suppose inviolate abstinence.[15]

While non-virgins may practise abstinence, they can never see themselves as virginal. In turn, virginity needs to be practised in the right spirit if it is to count as *true* virginity. For virginity can only be called 'Christian ... where celibacy is undertaken for the sake of the kingdom of Heaven'.[16] The implication here is also that real, authentic virginity can only ever be Christian virginity. The same writer also argues that virginity in the sense espoused by the early Church applies equally to both men and women, and that it means 'total and undivided surrender to the Lord', both body and soul.[17] Virginity, understood in this sense, represents for Christians both the original state of humans before the Fall and the radical transformation of the New Testament. Whereas for Rabbinic Judaism marriage represented a 'moral obligation', Christians see Christ's life as a sign of the new order in which lifelong virginity 'became a possible vocation and a legitimate and blessed way of life, for the kingdom of heaven's sake'.[18] Dedicated virginity therefore is 'a call to perfection'.[19] In their renunciation of human love and human relationships, Christian virgins also exemplify virginity's sacrificial nature. Because it is vowed, lifelong virginity 'means . . . the perpetual sharing in the Cross of Christ'; it is to be understood as 'an unbloody, but lifelong martyrdom'.[20]

Virgins and wives

With the development of canon law – ecclesiastical law – and a growing interest in the governing and control of sexuality in the twelfth century, it is not surprising that virginity and marriage – representative of the 'spiritual' and the 'worldly' respectively – were defined in relation to one another. In medieval religious texts there are three states of womanhood that are acceptable: virginity, widowhood and marriage, each with its own reward in heaven. Of these three, virginity is the highest state and marriage the lowest, for marriage should be thought of as 'a bed for the sick, to catch those who are not strong' enough to resist their sexual urges.[21] Widows, however, can repent of and confess their sexual deeds, which raises them up to a state of 'chaste purity', second only to virginity. Medieval writers extolling the virtues of a virginal life often chose to focus on the positive aspects of renouncing worldly relationships, particularly those of marriage and motherhood. Following a long and established tradition of virginity treatises reaching back to the third or fourth century AD, *Holy Maidenhood* is explicit in its depiction of what awaits the woman who chooses to bind herself to a husband: 'He rebukes you, rails at you and humiliates you disgracefully, he takes you shamefully as a lecher his whore, strikes you and beats you as his bought slave and born serf'. Even in the (unlikely) event of the marriage turning out to be a happy one, the author warns the virgin that pregnancy will 'distend you like a water-bag' and turn your face 'thin' and as 'green as grass'. Domestic life, the author concludes, is hellish:

> And what if I go on to ask . . . what life is like for the woman who, when she comes in, hears her children screaming, sees the cat at the bacon and the dog at the rind, her cake burning on the hearth and her calf sucking spilt milk, the pot boiling over in the fire – and the lout grumbles away?

The woman who chooses a life of dedicated virginity 'escape[s] from such slavery'; she is 'God's free daughter'.[22]

The decision to remain a virgin was, in aristocratic circles at least, a serious choice for a woman whose family often viewed her as a bargaining chip on the table of financial negotiations. Lucrative marriage contracts could be jeopardized if the daughter in question decided to become a bride of Christ rather than of some nobleman. One account of this is found in the twelfth-century life of Christina of Markyate. Written by an anonymous monk at St Albans at around the same time that the Gilbertines were being investigated for alleged sexual misconduct, the story tells of a young aristocratic woman who has chosen to dedicate herself to Christ after her parents took her on a visit to the monastery of St Alban. Her vow is confirmed by a local priest and marks the beginning of many trials and tribulations. When her parents want her to marry a young nobleman called Burthred, Christina refuses, citing her vow of virginity as the reason. Outraged at her refusal of this socially advantageous match, her parents reproach her, isolate her from friends and attempt to bribe her. Under all of this pressure, Christina agrees to a betrothal but refuses to consummate the marriage. The parents resume their harrying, trying to tempt her away from the path of purity by taking her to parties, feasts and amusements of all kinds, as well as trying to get her drunk. Eventually, they hit on the plan of letting Burthred into her room one night so that he can consummate the marriage by raping her. Christina tries to convince him that they should live together chastely, but when he is mocked for not being man enough by those waiting outside, he returns, determined to violate her. After much more ill-treatment by her family, Christina finally manages to escape by disguising herself as a man. With the help of other religious women and men, who hide and support her, she eventually becomes a revered holy woman.

Here virginity functions as a symbol for the respective – and often conflicting – demands and powers of religious and secular institutions. Christina's father is said to be angry because his daughter is 'depart[ing] from tradition' and bringing 'dishonour' on him;[23] he sees her vow of virginity as an affront to his patriarchal authority. On the other hand, what is being asserted here is the supremacy of *God*'s patriarchal authority over any human. Christina has promised herself to him with a vow – a vow that was held to be as binding as any marriage vow – and therefore she could claim that her subsequent betrothal to Burthred did not count. This is reminiscent of the story of the Nun of Watton who, when she meets with her lover, is called an 'adulteress' by Aelred. As a dedicated nun, she is married to Christ and has betrayed him as if he were her husband. Her loss of virginity is an act of infidelity to the best husband of all.

From a theological standpoint, Christianity has the power to redefine the significance of human relationships. Understood in this sense, the Christian community rather than biological kinship makes up one's 'true' family, while 'true' love or marriage is the love of Christ, rather than love for another person.[24] In this view, Christ is the superlative husband, and the frequent use of nuptial imagery in religious writings serves to highlight not only how dedicating one's virginity to Christ is parallel to (but better than) sacrificing one's life to someone in marriage, but also encourages a comparison between the flawed human spouse and the sublime heavenly one. While later Catholic writers tend to underline the holiness and dignity of marriage, stating that 'Christian marriage is a holy state', in a direct comparison virginity is still said to be 'objectively more perfect'; a 'greater, more sublime mystery'.[25]

In his third-century treatise 'On the Veiling of Virgins', Tertullian, writing in Carthage in North Africa, argues that virgins must be veiled in the same way that non-virginal women are, as both belong to the same sex. If one were to deny this, the virgin would become 'a third generic class, a monstrosity with a head of its own'.[26] Tertullian is clearly responding anxiously and defensively to the idea that virginity might offer women a way of escaping patriarchal control and rule. While on the one hand religious writers reminded young women of the tribulations they could avoid if they chose a virginal career, on the other the religious establishment did not want to promote the idea that women who chose a life of virginity could expect a greater degree of independence from male supervision or authority. Religious writings from the twelfth century onwards increasingly portray the female virgin not as the masculinized virago, casting aside her female nature, but as the feminized bride of Christ. The idea of the soul in general and of the female virgin in particular as a bride of Christ has a long history in Western Christianity, beginning around the fourth century AD, and is invoked by writers such as Augustine, Ambrose and Tertullian.[27]

A woman's entry into the religious life was celebrated as a nuptial rite, revealing a concern with maintaining the differences between men and women. These differences gave each sex clearly defined and hierarchically ordered roles in society. As one religious writer in the twentieth century explains in the same vein, men and women dedicated to a religious life must still perform different roles, just as they do in secular life: 'Man's task at home is to rule; the priest's task in the Church is to preside and direct. This is not woman's role; on the contrary, St Paul exhorts her to be submissive.'[28] The female virgin must not presume to teach or to speak; her 'spiritual fruitfulness is derived from her silence and solitude'. Here, virginity is understood as essentially more feminine, a more accurate reflection of women's than men's nature:

This aspect of the mystery of virginity . . . is based on an essential aspect of feminine nature: in fact woman is a being with a sense of needing something; she seeks a support, a protector, a head. She is aware of her insufficiency, and has an innate need to dedicate herself, to belong to someone.[29]

While the last point can then be extended to apply to all of humanity – for all of humanity exists in a relationship of need for and reliance on the God the Creator – women exemplify this twice over: in the order ordained by God on earth, they must rely on and obey men as well as God. So although a woman can be the most apt symbol for the lofty mystery of virginity, her innate frailty means that she still cannot claim independence from male authority:

Women's affective life is full of pitfalls, feelings, sentimentality, and the rest, even when in good faith she has Christ for the object of her affections . . . [T]hat is why the Church keeps watch through her bishops, priests and theologians, who are men.[30]

And just in case we haven't understood that although female virgins *are* special they offer nothing new or authoritative, it is firmly reiterated that '[t]he virgin of Christ brings us no new way, she has nothing to add to what the hierarchy of bishops and priests imparts to us'. It is also made clear that the decision to live a life of true virginity is not something that can be made by the individual on her own. As this writer puts it, 'Faith is a grace, virginity likewise'.[31] It is precisely this emphasis on God's grace that made lifelong and vowed virginity seem such a precarious and unlikely achievement to Protestant reformers.

Reformed virginity

Martin Luther (1483–1546), John Calvin (1509–64) and other reformers objected to the taking of the vow of celibacy or virginity – to them, the majority of those taking the vow could not truly hope to keep it and therefore were making a mockery both of virginity *and* marriage. The danger was that those who had taken it without a true vocation would act on their sexual urges outside the bounds of marriage. In 'The Estate of Marriage' (1522), Luther makes it clear that marriage is the universal condition that men and women have to conform to, for it 'is a matter of nature and not of choice'. If it is resisted, the results are 'fornication, adultery and secret sins'.[32] It is not virginity itself that was attacked by reformers, but the alleged abuses of it, as well as its elevation to the highest state by Catholicism. While the emphasis in post-Reformation Protestant thought clearly did shift from the Virgin Mary to Christ, the question of purity remained important; the difference was that it was the purity of Christ that was underlined now, rather than the Immaculate Conception or the Virgin Birth.[33] It was not, Protestant and Puritan writers pointed out, the Virgin Mary herself who was under attack, but the manner in which she had been worshipped by Catholics who, they believed, had turned her into an idol.[34]

The cult of the Virgin Mary was indubitably one of the most popular in the Middle Ages, and 'no other figure played such multiple roles in people's devotional lives'. A more human, less remote figure than God or even Christ, her maternal tenderness combined with her virginal innocence to make her appear a merciful intercessor in the eyes of many believers, both male and female. Because she was mother, daughter, wife and maiden, the qualities associated with each of these roles

An engraving of the blessed Virgin Mary, depicting the mother of God as a young and beautiful woman, eyes modestly downcast.

were attributed to Mary. In addition, because she was Christ's mother, she possessed authority and commanded respect. Her many virtues are expressed poignantly in the *Salve regina*, dating from the eleventh century:

Hail queen and mother of mercy,
Hail our life, comfort, and hope.
Exiled children of Eve, we cry to you.
We sigh weeping and wailing to you,
In this valley of tears.
Come then, our advocate,
And turn those eyes of pity towards us now,
When this time of exile is past,
Show us Jesus, the blessed fruit of your womb,
O clement, O pious, O sweet Virgin Mary.[35]

While Marian devotion began in the monasteries in the twelfth century, it quickly spread and was taken up enthusiastically by the laity. Within religious writings, Mary was often exalted as the ideal pattern on which women should model their own lives – a difficult challenge considering Mary's exceptional status as virgin-mother. As St Ambrose, that most passionate proponent of virginity, wrote in the fourth century to the virgin Marcellina:

Let, then, the life of Mary be as it were virginity itself, set forth in a likeness, from which, as from a mirror, the appearance of chastity and the form of virtue is reflected. From this you may take your pattern of life, showing, as an example, the clear rules of virtue: what you have to correct, to effect, and to hold fast.[36]

Incidents from Mary's life (such as the Annunciation, the Nativity and her Assumption) were celebrated on official feast days, as well as being recounted – along with many more stories of miracles and praises of her virtue – in devotional writings, literature, architecture, stained glass, sculpture and music. This devotion to Mary still endures today. Her popularity may well have caused concern even before the Reformation, as it threatened to draw attention away from God.

Yet while it is commonly known that the Reformation and Protestant denominations since then have tended to focus on marriage rather than virginity as the most natural and God-willed state for humans on earth, it is less well known than virginity *per se* was not denigrated, nor did it lose its exalted status. Citing Matthew 19:12, Luther argues in 'The Estate of Marriage' that God has exempted only three categories of men from this otherwise universal injunction: those who have been eunuchs 'from birth', those who 'have been made eunuchs by men' and, lastly those 'who have made themselves eunuchs for the sake of the kingdom of heaven'. For Luther, the majority of nuns and monks who took the vow of celibacy did not fit these categories, least of all the last one:

> The third category consists of those spiritually rich and exalted persons, bridled by the grace of God, who are equipped for marriage by nature and physical capacity and nevertheless voluntarily remain celibate . . . Such persons are rare, not one in a thousand.[37]

Similarly, that other great reformer, Calvin, though in many ways very different from Luther, also did not simply dismiss the state of virginity. Drawing on St Paul, he voiced the familiar argument that celibacy and virginity allowed an individual more freedom to contemplate and strive towards God. And, 'finally, marriage is a remedy ordained by God to help our weakness, and is to be used by anyone who does not possess the gift of continence.'[38]

In a sense, then, virginity – at least lifelong virginity or virginity as profession – was *further* rarefied by Protestantism. Now considered so difficult a feat that only the very few could possibly hope to strive for and achieve it – and then only by God's grace – it was edged to the margins. Instead, marriage was increasingly praised as the 'natural' state, and Protestant writings are full of suspicions cast on the Catholic ordinance of chastity and virginity for those dedicated to a religious life. Claims to lifelong virginity by members of the clergy were treated with scepticism, even derision, as they were suspected to be a mere cover for unbridled fornication and other unspeakable acts of excess. Stories proliferated about nuns having abortions and drowning the foetuses in monastic ponds, burying them in cellars or eating abortifacient leaves of trees and plants grown for that purpose around monastic buildings.

While it is impossible to claim that there was any absolute post-Reformation Protestant stance towards virginity, the Catholic Church's Counter-Reformation was swift in its response to Protestantism's perceived promotion of marriage over virginity. In the Council of Trent (1563) under Pope Pius IV, it was declared in the tenth of the 'Canons on the Sacrament of Matrimony' that: 'If anyone saith that the marriage state is to be placed above the state of virginity, or of celibacy, and that it is not better and more blessed to remain in virginity, or in celibacy, than to be united in matrimony; let him be anathema.'[39] As early as the later sixteenth century, it seems that England witnessed a revival of the praise for holy virginity – even for Mariolatry. While writers such as Thomas More or Desiderius Erasmus were highly critical of celibacy or maintained virginity, it is clear that others, even Protestants, still saw much to applaud.[40] One such writer was Thomas Bentley who, in *The Monument of Matrons: conteining seuen seuerall Lamps of Virginitie* (1582), 'eulogises [Queen] Elizabeth as a perpetual virgin in a fashion not found in earlier years'.[41] Bentley's collection includes a number of prayers, to be used by 'all sorts and degrees of women', and those specific to 'single women' are meant to help them fend against 'all evil behaviour, vice, and vanity' and to enable them to maintain (or obtain) 'modesty, chastity, and all maidenly virtues'. These are not prayers written for women who have vowed life-long virginity, or who have dedicated themselves to a religious vocation. Nonetheless, they outline the importance of virginity (and the dangers to it) in very similar terms to those used in medieval guides written for religious women. Bentley gives a very good idea of exactly how precarious and fragile a state virginity was still considered to be – both physically and spiritually – when he lists the seemingly endless 'snares of Satan' the virgin must avoid if she hopes to maintain the 'inestimable treasure' of her virginity:

> [B]anquets, weddings, idle games, heathenish sports, & dissolute plays, and pastimes, vain pleasures, and filthy dalliance and dancings, the extreme of all vices: finally, from all envy, arrogance, ambition, impudence, pertness, boldness, rashness, unshamefastness, dissolute laughing, excessive feeding, recklessness, dissoluteness, deliciousness, wantonness, lightness, inconstancy, curiosity . . . [42]

In another passage he clearly supports the view that matrimony is for those who cannot stand the rigours of a virginal life, and the images he uses to refer to virginity are identical to those used by such earlier, Catholic, texts as *Holy Maidenhood*.

The stronger the animosities between Catholic and Protestant – as demonstrated by, for instance, the Northern Rebellion led by English Catholics (1569) or the St Bartholomew's Day Massacre in Paris (1572) – the more extreme the vilification of what were perceived as differences of faith, particularly the status of the Virgin Mary. At the same time, virginity or virginal purity were claimed by both Protestants and Catholics at various times and in various ways in order to legitimize their respective religious and political agendas. While later reformers eventually moved away from the view expressed by Luther and Calvin, its influence is discernible in the thought of some later Protestant radical groups, such as the English Ranters in the seventeenth century, or the Shakers, who originated in Manchester and went to America to escape persecution in the eighteenth century.

For some Protestant thinkers, the female virgin even came to stand for 'the specifically seventeenth-century image of the autonomous liberal self', and was linked to calls for 'individual human rights'. Some critics suggest that political uses of the concept of virginity are evidence that England witnessed an 'elevation of the sustained life of virginity to a moral ideal' at this time. The renewed interest in virginity turned it into a 'political principle', available to 'Catholics and Protestants, republicans . . . Royalists', to fringe groups as well as mainstream Anglican theologians.[43] For the more radical groups, virginity's appeal lay in what was seen to be its apocalyptic symbolism. Those who remained virgins could dedicate themselves to the 'eschatological union of heaven and earth' as described in Revelation 14:1–5, which asserts that those 'redeemed from the earth' at the end are those who 'were not defiled with women: for they are virgins'.[44] Gerrard Winstanley, leader of the seventeenth-century English radical dissenters known as Diggers, explains in *Fire in the Bush* that each believer will be returned to a prelapsarian state of innocence (a condition he describes as 'the Virgin-state of Mankind') by Christ at the end of time. Drawing on the example of Mary, Winstanley describes the virgin state in which humanity and Christ will be united at the Second Coming:

> This chaste Virgin-state, that hath no outward Lover, and that is not Defiled, but cleansed from deformity, is this Virgin chaste state, in whom the Son of righteousness will arise, and take the man into union with himself[.][45]

In an anonymous treatise called *A Looking-Glasse for the Ranters* (1653) we find the argument that those who praise and extol the institution of marriage have, in fact, got it all wrong. In the part entitled 'A Treatise of Virginity', it is stated that 'Virgins only are a Bride for the Bridegroom Jesus Christ' and that many have misinterpreted God's command to be fruitful and multiply. In the view put forward by this writer, God made Adam in his own image, and therefore fruitfulness is to be understood in purely spiritual terms: 'In the beginning God made all good, pure, and perfect, the man and woman were so in their first condition' and 'they should be kept chaste Virgins in God, and so fructify'.[46] Virgins are the only ones who can bear Christ within themselves, and so only virgins will be able to bear God's word and produce spiritual offspring. Furthermore, those 'that act in the flesh are by Law excluded [from] the Kingdom of God', for '*God cannot love that which is unlike himself*'. The overall framework is an apocalyptic one: the wise virgins will 'enter with [Christ] into his Glory'; they die 'daily with Christ, to live with him eternally'. Those who truly desire God's word 'do abstain from fleshly lusts . . . [and] abstain, wait, watch long for, and labour if by any means they may attain resurrection from the dead'.[47]

As this brief outline shows, attitudes towards virginity were far from clear-cut. The potency of virginity and the ideals it was believed to embody were drawn on by theological writers both Protestant and Catholic, in a range of different ways. At the same time, while these groups existed, they did not accurately reflect the general mood, particularly in later centuries. The Puritans, for instance, were unequivocal in their opposition to monastic forms of life, and also denied the superiority of virginity or celibacy to marriage. Like Luther and Calvin, the Puritans criticized the enforced nature of lifelong celibacy in a monastic environment, where purity was ensured by locking men and women away from the world and by demanding a vow from them. In contrast, Puritans developed the idea of an 'inner conscience' that, properly trained, would enable the individual to be in control of his/her emotions and interactions with others at all times. Here, emphasis is on the individual person: on control from within the self.[48] Yet virginity stubbornly re-emerges time and time again in the ideals pursued by less mainstream Protestant groups, even those whose roots were clearly Puritan. In fact, some Protestant offshoots and sects had an ongoing love affair with virginity, one which is arguably becoming more visible again today, particularly in the US.

In the nineteenth century, dramatic and rapid social change

affected the organization of the family and the roles of men and women within families in fundamental ways. Three American sects which experimented with different familial and sexual models were the Shakers, the Mormons and the Oneida Perfectionists. As one critic sums it up: 'the Shakers are known for their celibacy, the Mormons for polygamy and reproductive abundance, and the Oneidans for free love and eugenics'.[49] They emerged in the mid-eighteenth century, after the revivalist movement known as the Great Awakening had swept swiftly through the American colonies, 'resulting in an unprecedented era of . . . doctrinal innovations' and 'divisions'. These groups articulated their aims within a millenarian framework, believing that 'the kingdom of God could be established on earth', and strove to recapture what they saw as the original purity of the early Church.[50] Doing this would act as an antidote to what they perceived to be the corruption and turmoil of the world and society they lived in. For the Shakers, celibacy and virginity were central features of the way in which they imagined this ideal community.

Although reliable information is scarce about the genesis of the Shaker sect in England, which is thought to have emerged in the seventeenth century, it is known to have come to America with the Mancunian Ann Lee in 1744, who acted as their leader. The Shakers believed in a God who possessed a nature both male and female. In their view, celibacy and virginity relieved women from the hazards and demands of childbearing and child-rearing, freeing them for equal participation in the spiritual life. Virginity was also a way of life that expressed the ideal of self-control in its fullest form; in conquering bodily desires, one triumphed over the lowest aspect of human nature.[51] Drawing on the trope of Christ as bridegroom, Lee urged those who wanted to marry, to marry Christ.[52] An 1884 treatise on Shaker beliefs by Giles B. Avery, *Sketches of Shakers and Shakerism: Synopsis of Theology of United Society of Believers in Christ's Second Appearing*, explains that '[t]he Shaker institution is a *theocracy*', since its members anticipated the second coming of Christ. In this theocracy, men and women are equal and one of its requirements is that members 'take up a daily cross against all the passions of a worldly, generative life, living a life of pure, virgin celibacy'. Purity is 'the way that leads to God'.[53] In a tract entitled 'A Shaker's Answer to the Oft-Repeated Question, "What Would Become Of the World If All Should Become Shakers?"' (1874), prominent Shaker R. W. Pelham points out that not all people are or indeed can be the same on earth: 'The great Architect has various grades of work-men, all necessary in their places, in order to carry on the work and complete the building.' In the same vein, diversity is used to counter the (by now common) accusation that abstinence was unnatural by arguing that the fact all creatures have the means of procreation does not mean that they must use them: 'The fact is plain: Nature has no law requiring the reproductive organs be used merely because they exist.' Going one step further, he pro-poses that, in fact, it is *virginity* that is natural to humans: virginity and continence are signs of a higher stage of evolution, both racially and mentally. He even predicts that 'the time will come that *reproduction will cease!*'[54]

More generally, however, the move was away from virgin-ity as vocation or lifelong state, even though the idealization of virginity and purity can still be discerned, particularly in the way women were viewed. In the eighteenth century, for instance, there was a shift in the way female nature was thought about, towards an ideal of asexual purity. Whereas, until then, women were thought to be the more sexually desiring of the two sexes, Puritan values helped to redefine the female sex as one marked by delicate refinement and sensibility. This development was linked to the growing emphasis on 'self-control', which made the 'purer' woman responsible for the man's more carnal nature. The new 'cult of true womanhood' depicted women as rarefied creatures: the keepers of both the family's and the nation's morality and purity. Women were the guardians of culture and civilization, and it was their role to help to 'tame' men and to raise children according to these values.[55]

Yet while women were effectively desexualized, the new ideal did not lead the overall culture to place a higher value on virginity or, rather, on *maintained* virginity. And while an emphasis on self-control may have been one of the outcomes of Puritanism, contrary to the common caricature of the uptight Puritan it was not one of its aims. Puritanism in fact not only praised marriage, but also encouraged mutual delight in sex within marriage. Yet now it was being asserted that women, by their very nature, did not want or enjoy sex. What women *did* want, it was claimed, was children; this, in fact, was their *raison d'être*, their true calling. Motherhood and wifehood were the roles that became increasingly upheld as natural to and desirable for women; maintained virginity could only provoke suspicion or even derision. Furthermore, as in other moments in history, the maintenance of virginity was viewed as potentially subversive, a challenge to the patriarchal order, since it was suspected that women might use virginity as a means of escaping the roles society prescribed for them. Even within marriage, it was suspected that women might take on the ideal of the asexual goddess of the household to their own advantage – especially if they wished to escape the sexual demands of their husbands and the rigours of childbirth.[56]

Passionate purity

Many of these elements – particularly the emphasis on self-control and virginity until marriage – are still at the centre of current conservative evangelical Protestant debate, particularly in the US. While the twentieth century may have witnessed a sexual revolution that radically questioned – and altered – the way sexuality is experienced and thought about, the influence of traditional religious views has never disappeared and, arguably, is stronger today than it has been for decades.[57] As Christian Smith argues:

> Evangelicals were virtually invisible on the radar screen of American public life prior to the mid-1970s. While numbering in the tens of millions and growing in adherents and institutional strength, American evangelicals had for decades blended into mainstream American life. But the 1976 election of the 'born-again' President Jimmy Carter and the rise in the late 1970s of Jerry Falwell's Moral Majority changed all of that. Evangelicals found themselves on the American cultural and political map, and they have remained throughout the decades since then.[58]

In recent years, George W. Bush's government – following what some have seen as Bill Clinton's initial support for abstinence education in the mid-1990s – has put virginity back on the agenda, claiming that doing so is part of its response to a widespread yearning for a return to 'traditional values'.

Although this is a nebulous term (which is undoubtedly part of its potency and success), there are numerous religious groups, thinkers and writers who express their views on sexuality and on virginity unambiguously in response to what they see as a corrupt and anarchic society. As the foreword to *A Passion for Purity: Protecting God's Precious Gift of Virginity* (2003) sombrely states: 'Never before have morals been ignored as much as they are today.'[59]

This is a theme that runs through the publications of other contemporary conservative evangelical writers and groups.[60] Elisabeth Elliot, author of, among many other books, the successful *Passion and Purity: Learning to Bring Your Love Life under Christ's Control* (1984), claims that contemporary Western society wilfully thinks it can do away with rules which structured gender, sexual, familial and social relationships for 'thousands of years':

> Somehow we've gotten the idea that we can forget all the regulations and get away with it. Times have changed, we say. We're 'liberated' at last from our inhibitions. We have Sex and the Single Girl now. We have freedom. We can, in fact, 'have it all and not get hooked.' Women can be predators if they want to, as well as men.

She despairs of the generation she is addressing:

> How shall I speak of a few careless kisses as sin to a generation nurtured on the assumption that nearly everybody goes to bed with everybody? Of those who flounder in the sea of permissiveness and self-indulgence, are there any who still search the sky for the beacon of purity?

But she concludes that there are those willing to listen to her message: 'If I did not believe there were, I would not bother to write'. She acknowledges that those who seek 'purity of heart' must be 'prepared to be thought very odd'. However, this 'oddness' will allow one to be included in a pure elite, who live in the way God originally intended: '[Purity] means cleanness, clearness – not additives, nothing artificial – in other words, "all natural," in the sense in which the Original Designer designed it to be'.[61]

In *A Passion for Purity*, Carla A. Stephens (who serves the Atlanta-based, non-denominational World Changers Church International) tells the female readers she is explicitly writing for that by following the models of female sexuality they see promoted around them in contemporary American culture, they 'sacrifice something that God treasures dearly – [their] virginity – and end up feeling confused, depressed, hurt, and rejected'. A result of the devaluation of virginity is that women today 'are completely unaware of their true value'. Virginity is a 'defense mechanism' against 'the strong forces of sexual temptation', a concept introduced by God himself ('who knows what is best for His creation') and exemplified by Christ's life. She tells women that they must realize that if they are born again in Christ, they no longer own their bodies: 'You gave up your rights when you became born again'. Elliot too seeks to convince her readership (male and female) that virginity and abstinence are God's gifts which, taken seriously, will lead to a more fulfilled life, either within marriage or as a lifelong celibate (depending on which God wants for the specific individual). Along the way, promiscuity, materialism, individualism, teen pregnancies, depression and alienation are heavily criticized as the legacy of our modern, secular age.

Part of the problem of the denigration of virginity, in Stephens' view, is that people misunderstand its true meaning, seeing it as a purely physical state, whereas in fact, 'when one remains sexually pure, her body and spirit join together as one unit to worship God'.[62]

Achieving or maintaining such a state, these writers agree, is difficult, but they offer strict guidelines. Elliot's book is succinct and clear about its agenda, basing its authority equally on God and on her own personal experience when meeting her first husband, a fellow evangelical: 'It is, to be blunt, a book about virginity. It is possible to love passionately and to stay out of bed. I know. We did it.' For Elliot, it is all about 'honor', another concept that she feels has 'largely been lost'. In her definition, honour is 'fidelity to a system of fixed values and relations', and demands a willingness to sacrifice oneself, to curb one's desires and urges. Unsurprisingly, self-discipline features strongly in the evangelical world-view. 'Natural' desires are acknowledged as '[a] good and perfect gift', but this only increases the necessity 'that they be restrained, controlled, corrected, even crucified, that they might be reborn in power and purity for God'. We should try to imitate Christ and this process requires '[a] lot of hammering and chiseling and purifying by fire'.[63]

Joshua Harris, a pastor at the 'reformed charismatic' Covenant Life Church in Maryland and bestselling author, outlines his personal transformation in *I Kissed Dating Goodbye* (1997). The decision to remain pure for Christ is shown to offer a whole trajectory of success. When Harris goes on a religious retreat in high school and realizes his own sinfulness, the transformation is swift and all-encompassing:

I repented of my sin right then, and when I got home from the retreat I threw away the pornographic magazines ... At the same time I quit the gymnastics team and got involved with my church's youth group. My next girlfriend was a Christian and we didn't even kiss. I became a student leader and gained a reputation as someone who was serious about his faith.[64]

Along the way, he discovers the 'peace and power that came from purity'. In other words, purity and virginity are not merely aspects of your sexual life, but fundamental to a whole outlook; an outlook that turns you away from selfish individualism to selfless concern for others; away from fleshly desires towards spiritual awakening and sharing. Although Christians 'may hold higher standards than [their] pagan neighbors', Harris laments that sexual intimacy is not respected sufficiently in the current climate, even among believers. And this is why dating is problematic: '[W]e've got to keep in mind that the system of dating as we know it grew out of a culture that celebrates self-centredness and immorality.'[65] For those who can no longer resist or transform sexual desires, marriage is the only option.[66]

For Harris, premarital sex not only goes against God's will that we all remain virginal until marriage; it also creates emotional baggage such as 'guilt and regret' that threaten the 'real' relationship of marriage. Focusing on sexual relationships (or on dating) too early results in the stunting of the young person's personality, social life and talents: 'Instead of serving in their local church, instead of equipping themselves with the character, education, and experience necessary to succeed in life, many allow themselves to be consumed by the present needs that dating emphasizes.'

Dating also distracts from marriage, since it offers a cosy 'limbo', which means that those enjoying its pleasures do not find it necessary to move on to marriage. In fact, it cannot even be seen as offering the individual experiences that will prepare him or her for the commitment of marriage; rather, 'it can be a training ground for divorce'. Even those who decide to remain virgins until marriage, but continue dating, are not truly committed to purity. In one of his examples, Harris tells us about sixteen-year-old Jessica, who is 'a good girl', committed to saving her virginity until marriage. The flaw is that she 'places herself in compromising situations with her older boyfriend'. Once she sees the light, however, she recognizes that 'purity consists of more than remaining a virgin'; she now knows that she must 'drastically change her lifestyle', since '[w]here, when, and with whom you choose to spend your time reveals your true commitment to purity'. Harris refers to this recognition as a 'revolution': virginity is radical. This means there is little – or no – room for halfway measures: 'True purity . . . is a direction, a persistent, determined pursuit of righteousness. This direction starts in the heart, and we express it in a lifestyle that flees opportunities for compromise.'[67]

Understood this way, virginity is not so much a fixed state or condition, as a journey one must undertake: 'We have to understand purity as a *pursuit* of righteousness . . . If we want to lead pure lives, then we must realize that purity does not happen by accident. Rather, we must constantly pursue the direction of purity.' Harris outlines the steps towards achieving a lifestyle dedicated to purity: as well as seeking 'godly' mentors, one should always be aware of and monitor outside influences – 'Who and what you listen to, read, and watch'. This might mean shutting out a large part of the world:

> [Y]ou need to stop reading romance novels and watching soap operas ... Perhaps you need to turn off the radio because much of today's music exalts a false definition of love. You might need to tune out of some of your favorite TV shows because they mock your beliefs about purity. Whatever tempts you toward discontentment or compromise, don't put up with it. Tune it out. Turn it off.[68]

At the same time one must also guard against the inner traitor: Christian friends, relatives and role models should be enlisted as aides in the battle against one's 'deceitful heart': '[P]icture guarding your heart as if your heart were a criminal tied in a chair who would like to break free and knock you over the head.'

Harris' solution to all questions concerning sexuality and relationships is rather simple, not to say simplistic, since for him all such issues are linked 'to adopting a fallen world's attitudes toward love'. This 'fallen' attitude presents sex as a commodity, and tells people that 'love is something beyond our control', which conveniently excuses us all 'from having to behave responsibly'. In this scenario, he makes little distinction between indulging in premarital sex and using love as an excuse for 'immorality, murder, rape, and many other sins'. Like Elliot and Stephens, Harris blames a lot of current sexual mores on a culture of immediate gratification: 'Our culture teaches us that if something is good, we should seek to enjoy it immediately. So we microwave our food, e-mail our letters, and express mail our packages.' Yet the only critique made as a result of this recognition is of dating. There is, for instance, no real acknowledgement of the problematic impact of economic factors and demands on relationship and social patterns. In fact, while on the one hand they critique the culture of instant gratification, on the other hand the explicit comparison of personal relationships with capitalist consumer patterns is prominent in both Stephens' and Harris' books. Harris claims at one point that '[t]he timing of many dating relationships is equivalent to going shopping for an outfit when you don't have any money',[69] while Stephens tells the reader to think of virginity as an alarm system in a 'house worth millions of dollars'.[70]

A different kind of link is made between virginity and economics when the single life is seen as a phase in which to prepare oneself for the responsibilities of marriage, emotional as well as financial. Remaining 'pure' in that single phase thus demonstrates control over one's carnal nature as well as the ability to control one's life in general. In this sense, virginity is valuable socio-economically as well. Harris claims that: 'Now is the time to learn how to budget, save, and tithe consistently . . . We need to make sure we don't develop patterns with money that will jeopardize a marriage or, even more important, waste God's resources.' All of this is part of a general outlook and life philosophy, presented under headings such as: 'What kind of lifestyle does God want us to pursue? What is His view of money and possessions?'[71] Virginity cannot be seen as separate from this wider context: it is an expression of a very specific and all-encompassing way of life.

Unsurprisingly, proscription and the dire consequences of sexual temptations and actions are highlighted in this kind of writing. This is particularly noticeable in some of the evangelical literature aimed at young people. *Revolve*, the US-based 'Biblezine' aimed at female teenagers, harbours within its glossy, teen-mag-style covers the New Testament, presented in colloquial, everyday language, with helpful notes and glosses. It also comes complete with fresh-faced, beautiful adolescents and colourful headlines and sections bearing titles such as 'Are You Dating a Godly Guy?' alongside others such as '100+ Ways to Apply Your Faith'. In its advice column 'Blab', it responds to concerned questions posed by adolescents, particularly about sex. It offers advice such as 'God wants Christians to marry other Christians', or 'it's not wrong for you to date if you are looking for a husband'.[72] It is also unequivocal in its view that '[h]omosexuality is clearly sinful' and that '[s]ex was designed for two people – a man and a woman'. Overall, sex is repeatedly linked to danger: dating a non-Christian is 'like playing with fire'; '[m]aking out is a really dangerous thing'; and masturbation is also best avoided since '[p]leasuring yourself . . . can lead you down the dangerous road of fantasizing, pornography, or wanting to try the real thing before marriage'.[73] It is clear that a condemnation of homosexuality (or any type of relationship that is not heterosexual marriage) and a clear division of gender roles for men and women are central to this outlook.

For Elliot, men and women's roles are fixed and unchanging: 'In the woman's [story], always the ancient longing – "And her desire shall be for a husband" . . . In the man's story, always the restlessness to wander, experiment, conquer.' And while both men and women are urged to remain virginal until marriage, the onus is clearly on the woman. In Elliot's view, the woman knows that she can control and manipulate a man's 'passions', while 'he will be as much of a gentleman as she requires'.[74] Thus, for her, as for many of the writers in the eighteenth century, the woman is *more* responsible and must guard both herself and the man who might be led to sin through her. The ever-efficient Harris clarifies what such an assessment means in practical terms by outlining the respective moral responsibilities of 'the guy' and the 'the girl'. Women demand particular attention, for both 'guys' and 'girls' are exhorted to watch over them: men must be vigilant, women self-vigilant. The 'guys', Harris tells us, must recognize that 'girls don't struggle with the same temptations' that men do, and must step up to fulfil their role as women's guardians:

> Guys, it's time we stood up to defend the honor and righteousness of our sisters. We need to stop acting like hunters trying to catch girls and begin seeing ourselves as warriors standing guard over them.

Not only are men protecting women for their own good, but they are protecting them for the good of other men: 'guys' must realize and they should aim to be the kind of man 'to whom girls' future husbands could one day say, "Thank you for guarding [my wife's] purity."' 'Girls' on the other hand, must acknowledge that they are always potentially temptresses: 'Remember the wayward woman we discussed earlier? Your job is to keep your brothers from being led astray by her charms.' In order to avoid being this kind of femme fatale themselves, they should combat sin by paying particular attention to their wardrobes: 'I would be blessed if girls considered more than fashion when shopping for clothes.' He recommends the actions of his friend, Janelle, who 'asks her dad to evaluate every outfit she buys. She wants a godly man's opinion of whether or not it's modest.'[75]

Homosexuality is either completely ignored by these writers, or alluded to indirectly, suggesting its 'unspeakable' status for evangelical Christianity. In order to illustrate that every person is potentially sinful, Harris relates an anecdote in which he is the object of homosexual desire. He passes a group of men who smile and wink at him. Initially puzzled by their attention, he suddenly realizes their intentions: 'I'll never forget the anger and disgust I felt at that moment . . . It was so wrong, so filthy. I remember turning to God in self-righteous anger and hissing through my clenched teeth, "Those people are so sick!"'[76] While the moral lesson of this anecdote is the recognition that 'smug heterosexual lust' is 'just as disgusting' in God's sight, the impact of the story is clearly meant to derive from outrage at such unnatural desire. The virginity of those not included in the heterosexual 'norm' is, unsurprisingly, not discussed at all and thus rendered non-existent. One teenager writing to *Revolve* for advice about being gay, is told ominously: 'Pray a lot. Ask God to give you repentance for your sin. And go talk to a Christian counselor – this is a big deal.'[77]

Essentially, these books are about one, exclusive model of relationship: heterosexual marriage. Marriage is the inevitable goal that all except those chosen by God to remain single are striving for. When one reaches marriageable age, the virginal, single phase should have allowed one to look around and seek out an appropriate spouse. Thus virginity is, for most people, the preparatory phase that leads to this final outcome, both physically and spiritually: 'God has a perfect plan for your life.

More than likely, that plan includes marriage, and if so, some-where in this world God has the perfect person for you.'[78]

Even if one falls, hope need not be lost, for virginity may be re-attainable. Disdaining the option of rehymenization through plastic surgery, some argue that it is possible to achieve 'revirginization'. Those who are 'separated, divorced, or widowed, or who have been sexually promiscuous' must go through a 'two-to-three year period of celibacy', after which they have gained their so-called 'secondary virginity'.[79] One website defines it more loosely: 'Secondary virginity, or being a "born-again" or "renewed" virgin, is when an individual who has had premarital sex chooses to "start again" and wait until marriage.'[80] In an article entitled 'A Renewed Virginity', posted on the website of *Christian Women Today*, progress towards regaining one's virginity is structured along a seven-step model, with headings such as 'Discover why you had sex so you can correct the problem'.[81] The site also offers inter-ested readers information on and links to other resources, for instance to 'faith-based resources to help parents guide their teens in making biblical choices about their sexuality'.

Virginity for religious writers in the twentieth- and twenty-first centuries, as for their predecessors, is both a physical and a spiritual state. The emphasis on lifelong virginity has clearly shifted, but the warnings about the slippery temptations of sex and the prescriptive nature of the advice have not. In addition, the Christian media offering information on virginity and sex-uality have also proliferated: books, magazines, websites, articles and talkshows abound. These sources also show that while virginity is still not seen as an absolute state – primarily because it can be threatened by sinful thoughts and not just concrete acts – much of the debate remains focused on the body. Perhaps the advice given to the teenager who wrote to *Revolve 2* asking 'How far can you go sexually before you are no longer pure?' can be offered as representative of contemporary conservative Protestant views of virginity and sex: 'Let's put it this way: How much dog poop stirred into your cookie batter does it take to ruin the whole batter?'[82]

3

'An Unknown Alphabet'

[V]irginity tells no story about itself but enables the story to be told.[1]

For neither it in Art nor Nature is . . .[2]

Beginnings

'In the beginning was the Word.' In the beginning there was also virginity. Adam and Eve were virgins, at a time of innocence, before the temptations of knowledge and the ensuing deception resulted in sexuality, shame, expulsion and death. Virginity is profoundly connected with narrative and origins in Western culture; it is the beginning of the story, before everything goes wrong. Or it is the ending, when all is resolved. Its maintenance or loss are what fuels innumerable plots; the resolution of stories about virgins tends to involve either marriage or death. Closely associated with both life and mortality, the virgin elicits desire and fear.

The ideals and qualities associated with virginity in Western literature in the past eight hundred years remain surprisingly constant, whether the story is set in 'the ancient Aegean, the

Roman court, the medieval countryside, or modern Los Angeles'.[3] It is not that there are no shifts in meanings surrounding this ideal, or that genres or contexts don't change, or that audiences didn't interpret virgin narratives differently. Rather, there is always a range of virginities present in writing at any given moment, and while these are not static, neither do they change so radically as to become unrecognizable or seem new. In Chaucer's *Canterbury Tales* alone, for instance, there are at least four different kinds of narrative treatments of virginity: in 'The Knight's Tale' we have Emily, an ethereal courtly romance heroine; in 'The Reeve's Tale' the miller's daughter is the type of earthy young woman familiar from bawdy tales; in 'The Monk's Tale' we meet Zenobia, a virgin warrior queen; and St Cecilia is the virgin martyr of 'The Second Nun's Tale'. How each story and genre represents the virgin varies, and sometimes these portrayals are incompatible: a virgin martyr does not act in the same way, or according to the same ideals, as the virgin heroine of a romance.[4] Equally, a writer might make a point of choosing a genre that was not thought to be appropriate to the topic of virginity. John Milton's use of the masque, which included music, dances and disguises, to launch a discussion of chastity was startling, since these kinds of dramatic entertainment were thought to be licentious.[5]

From the Middle Ages until today, virginity in literature has been represented in a variety of at times contradictory ways. Perhaps more fundamentally, this underlines the way virginity raises some of the same questions as literature: how is it to be read? Who is able to discern its signs and meanings? Who can interpret correctly? Is it a truthful narrative, or does it seduce its readers with falsehoods and empty promises? Is it original or counterfeit? Is it natural or self-consciously artful? Is it wholesome or sinful?

The pen and the page

Drawing on religious traditions that associated virginity with truth and also, as we saw in the last chapter, with the apocalypse, some authors emphasize the need to be either virginal or chaste themselves in order to be able to understand the truths they long to capture in writing. In his poem 'The Interpreters', John K. Ingram (1823–1907) aligns the poet with the saint, as mouthpiece for the divine, when he says that the Virgin Mary 'ordains as her Interpreters' both '[t]he mighty bard' and the 'meek saint'.[6] Through these 'rarer spirits of our race' she will 'speak her oracles'; others can thereby gain access to her mercy. Milton, representing a Protestant position that praised 'personal chastity' over maintained virginity, saw it as a 'necessary precondition for composing poetry'.[7] The purity of the writer makes him a worthy vessel, signalling his striving towards a righteous life in keeping with God's commands.

Far more frequent, however, is the comparison of the act of literary creation with sexual seduction. In a poem by Oliver Wendell Holmes (1809–94), 'To a Blank Sheet of Paper', production and reproduction are both performed on a virginal body:

> Wan-visaged thing! thy virgin leaf
> To me looks more deadly pale
> Unknowing what may stain thee yet, —
> A poem or a tale.[8]

This relationship – between 'virgin' page and creator/author – is a heavily gendered and sexualized one: the 'virgin leaf' is, like the female virgin, as yet unmarked by man, whose mark is a sign of possession and mastery. By using the word 'stain', the poet is deliberately evoking the image of the blood-stained white sheet that functions as 'proof' of the bride's virginity, and emphasizes the page's – and the virgin's – passivity: 'Unknowing what may stain thee yet'. Creation is defloration.

The unidentified poet known as 'Ephelia' draws a playful and bawdy comparison between writing a poem and loss of virginity in 'Maidenhead: Written at the Request of a Friend', first published in 1647.[9] It is the maidenhead itself as topic that acts as the stimulus for the poetic creation; the speaker tells us that she has finally given in to a friend's 'Intreaty' to write about it. At the end of the poem, the speaker laments mockingly:

> But I forget, or have my Subject lost:
> Alas! thy Being's Fancy at the most:
> Though much desired, 'tis but seldom Men
> Court the vain Blessing from a Womans Pen.

Her disorientation as a writer suggests that it parallels her loss of 'Subject' – both literarily and physically. The ending is more opaque, however. Is the poem saying that virginity is nothing but an illusion, though one that is 'much desired'? And why don't men want the blessing from a 'Womans Pen'? If the act of writing is likened to the act of defloration, one can see that the gendering makes the concept of a 'woman's pen' a problematic one. After all, can she be both virgin page *and* deflowerer?

One of the most famous and influential medieval texts is the thirteenth-century *Roman de la Rose* (*The Romance of the*

A miniature (*c.* 1490–1500) depicting the moment in *The Romance of the Rose* when the female figure of Fair Welcome leads the lover to the 'rose' that he desires to 'pluck'.

Rose), a dream-vision allegory that tells of a dreamer and would-be lover's journey along the path of courtly love, culminating in his 'plucking' of the 'rose'. This climactic defloration is preceded by a sermon given by Genius, who berates those who do not make use of the 'assets' Nature has given them:

It was an evil day for Nature when she gave stylus and tablets to those false folk of whom I have spoken, and hammers and anvils according to her laws and customs, and sharp-pointed ploughshares fit for her ploughs, and fallow fields, not stony ones but fertile and grassy, which need tilling and digging if they are to be enjoyed.[10]

Because these 'tools' are said to be given by Nature, the division of labour outlined here is automatically 'naturalized', which makes it seem like the norm, the way things are 'meant to be'. It thus represents the correct order of things, and any infringement or different model put forward becomes 'unnatural', a deviation.

The sexual roles of men and women outlined by Genius are not just divided into an active and a passive role (stylus writes on tablet; hammer pounds the anvil; plough tills the fecund field), but also in terms of work and creation. Genius excoriates 'those who will not use their styluses, through which mortals may live forever, to write on those fair and precious tablets'. Reproduction and writing ensure the survival and continuation of the human race – the former because it brings forth new humans, the latter because it records human deeds that then live on in the collective memory. Put more clearly: writing/fucking is done by men, on the bodies of women, and those who do not fulfil that role are cursed by Genius: 'May they be robbed of their styluses, since they refused to write with them on the precious tablets fit for that purpose!'[11] Centuries later, in the film *The Sound of Music* (1965), the young Nazi Rolf draws on this analogy of the virgin and the blank page when he sings to Liesl of her awakening sexuality in the song 'Sixteen Going on Seventeen':

> You wait, little girl, on an empty stage
> For fate to turn the light on
> Your life, little girl, is an empty page
> That men will want to write on.

Liesl, starry-eyed, sighs out the last line as a refrain, 'To write on', passively echoing his words. The song reduces the 'little girl's' life to an act of waiting that relies on another to awaken it and give it a narrative. Virgins tell no story about themselves, they await the man who will bring them to life by providing the active principle: light, writing, meaning. According to Rolf, Liesl needs someone to hand her a script. The virginal woman in these analogies is not just passive, she is also unformed matter, raw material awaiting the inscription, transformation, cultivation, that is presented as men's business.

A story that takes this idea to its logical extreme is that of Pygmalion, the renowned artist who falls in love with his own creation. It is unsurprising to find it among the stories the narrator of *The Romance of the Rose* draws on in the final chapter, before the rosebud is prised open by the dreamer. In order to 'put his great skill to the test . . . and to win renown',[12] Pygmalion fashions the figure of a woman out of ivory. This act of creation backfires, however, when he falls desperately in love with this image, dressing her in gorgeous, costly clothes, bringing her gifts of shoes, flowers and jewellery. The lengthy description that the *Romance* gives of his obsession with her focuses almost exclusively on the artfulness with which he makes and decorates her, as well as the songs he plays to her so skilfully. Here, artistic creation and the art of love are inseparable, and Pygmalion is ultimately rewarded by Venus, who listens to his prayers and breathes life into the sculpture. He is therefore, in a sense, both his creation's progenitor and suitor; if sex and art are claimed as masculine prerogatives, Pygmalion is both father and lover.[13]

Classical stories are repeatedly used to make such analogies. The power of the father over the daughter as his creation is laid out starkly by Theseus, Duke of Athens, in Shakespeare's

A Midsummer Night's Dream, when he tells Hermia that she has no right to choose her own husband, but must obey her father Egeus' wishes:

> Be advised, fair maid.
> To you your father should be as a god,
> One that composed your beauties; yea, and one
> To whom you are but as a form in wax
> By him imprinted, and within his power
> To leave the figure, or disfigure it.[14]

Here the father is the sole author of his daughter – she is nothing but his 'imprint'. Like Pygmalion's sculpture, she is his to do with as he pleases, even if that means destroying her. Hermia has fallen in love with the 'wrong' man, not the one her father has chosen for her; the power struggle here is between one kind of 'imprinter' and another. In this structure, it is through sex – and marriage – that the virgin passes from the possession of her father to that of her lover/husband.

While the role of the father might have changed in more recent literature, the act of defloration is still frequently represented in terms of a male asserting his ownership over virgin territory, especially in popular romance. In *The Sheikh's Virgin*, a recent Mills and Boon novel, Keira, the virginal heroine, is forced by her 'Barakan' father to undergo a physical examination to ensure that she is still intact before he marries her off to a 'radical fundamentalist'. The examination is prevented at the last moment by the appearance of the dashing Sheikh Kalen Nuri, who wants to prevent this marriage for his own political and personal reasons. He arrives, snarling, 'I will kill the man that touches what is mine', and marries Keira.[15]

Similarly, in *The Disobedient Virgin*, the successful American businessman Jake Ramirez, a self-made millionaire from the 'mean streets of the South Bronx', finds out after his father's death that the identity of the two half-brothers he never knew he had will only be revealed to him if he fulfills the conditions of his father's will. This means looking after the orphan Caterina, who has grown up in a hidden-away convent school in Brazil, until she is twenty-one, at which point he is to find her a suitable husband. The titillation in this plot arises from the juxtaposition of a twenty-first century setting and Caterina's child-like innocence and helplessness. She might be spirited, but she is also passed on from one man to the next without any real say in the matter. It is not long before Jake cannot bear the idea that another man will take that innocence, and explicitly associates its taking with possession of Caterina herself: 'Taking Caterina's virginity would ruin her for another man ... He'd have to stop before he slid deep inside her, before he took her maidenhead, before he made her his, only his.'[16] In *The Greek's Innocent Virgin*, Sebastian Kouros 'savoured the essence of Rachel with a consuming need to imprint himself on her, to make her know she was his.' As he is about to make love to her for the first time, he realizes that, '[t]he thought of another man doing to her what he was about to do was intolerable. "You are mine," he growled, as her tightness allowed him to gain only the beginning of an entry.'[17]

Bernardo Bertolucci's film *Stealing Beauty* (1996) combines an exploration of the triangular father-daughter-lover relationship with that of the association between sexual and artistic production. Lucy is a young American who goes to Italy to find out who her father is, as well as hoping to lose her virginity. She stays in the beautiful home of Diana and Ian, an English couple who are friends of her deceased poet mother, where she meets other visitors, such as the dying writer Alex. Ian is a brooding artist, who painted Lucy's mother's portrait years ago. The parallel narrative to this search for a father is the loss of Lucy's virginity, her 'journey into womanhood', as the cover of the DVD puts it. Lucy, nineteen years old, beautiful, innocent-yet-seductive, galvanizes all around her. Desire throbs in the hot summer air. All the men (except Diana's son, Christopher, who we later realize is gay) desire her in one way or another, and, while she has her own puzzle to solve, others perceive her as an intriguing mystery – mainly because of her virginity, which makes her an unknown quantity. Throughout the film she is connected to art in numerous ways: she is the daughter of a poet, a model for Ian, the muse for Alex and a budding writer herself. In the end, it becomes clear that Ian is, in fact, her true father: knowledge of her progenitor arrives simultaneously with the completion of the sculpture he has made of her and is followed by her loss of virginity – to Oswaldo, who is also a virgin, and deeply in love with her. It is as if discovering her father has enabled her to move into adulthood, and to recognize who her most genuine suitor is.

Much literature on virginity is about its loss: either through rape, unscrupulous seduction, love, marriage or death. Often it is art and artfulness that are presented as the tools of seduction. As Hermia's father, Egeus, says bitterly to Lysander:

> Thou, thou, Lysander, thou hast given her rhymes,
> And interchanged love-tokens with my child.

> Thou hast by moonlight at her window sung
> With feigning voices verses of feigning love,
> And stolen the impression of her fantasy[.][18]

Written several decades after Shakespeare's comedy, Philip Ayres's poem 'Love a Ticklish Game' playfully tells us that in order to catch virgin prey, the hunter must be artul:

> Virgins are like the silver finny Race
> Of slippery kind, and fishes seeme in part,
> Lovers looke to't; Be sure to bait the place,
> Lay well your Hookes, and cast your nets *with Art*.[19]

The reader can take from this either that the nets must be cast with skill, or that the 'Art' referred to is, in fact, poetry itself, with which one can ensnare the 'slippery' virgins.

The writer has power not just over the virgin page, but also over the virgin reader. Oliver Wendell Holmes conflates the two, by stating that whatever he chooses to 'stain' the virgin page with will equally affect the reader, making her (or him?), like the page, a reflection of his artistic choices:

> If it should be in pensive hour
> Some sorrow-moving theme I try,
> Ah, maiden, how thy tears will fall,
> For all I doom to die!

> But if in merry mood I touch
> Thy leaves, then shall the sight of thee
> Sow smiles as thick on rosy lips
> As ripples on the sea.[20]

There are many poems that exhort virgins more directly to remember that they will not be young and desired for ever, seeking to persuade them to relinquish their modesty for passion. The motif of *carpe diem* ('seize the day') engages in a mode of seduction in which virginity is merely the starting point and the narrative revolves around the 'will-she/won't-she' tease. This is perhaps most famously seen in Robert Herrick's 'To the Virgins, to Make Much of Time' (1648), which opens with the exhortation, 'Gather ye Rose-buds while ye may', and ends with the warning that life moves towards either death or the danger of being left on the shelf:

> Then be not coy, but use your time,
>   And while ye may go marry:
> For having lost but once your prime,
>   You may for ever tarry.[21]

Andrew Marvell offers the stark warning to his 'coy mistress' that, should she tarry too long, no one but death will be left to ravish her:

> . . . then worms shall try
> That long preserved virginity:
> And your quaint honor turn to dust,
> And into ashes all my lust.[22]

It is not surprising that moralists suspected narratives of love and seduction of sowing the seeds of moral corruption in 'impressionable' youthful readers. As the narrator in *The Romance of the Rose* points out, younger women are easier to fool with artful words, because they lack experience and knowledge of the wiles of men. Older women, on the other hand, 'are quicker to recognize lying talk than are the gentle maidens who can listen to flatterers without suspecting treachery, and who believe falsehoods and insincerities as if they were gospel'.[23] Similarly, in 'Advice to a Virgin', the seventeenth-century poet Thomas Heyrick lists the virgin's familiar attributes – 'beautiful', 'unexperienced' – adding that they are 'without defence', except for that provided by their innocence. This, however, is also problematic, as the virgin '[j]udges all things good' because she herself is good, unaware of 'what Dangers Thee surround, / What Plots and Stratagems [are] laid under ground' by 'fond Lovers'. He sets out to protect virgins from such plots by telling them simultaneously what it is that makes them desirable, and what it is they will lose should they succumb:

> For barren Countries none will ever fight,
> 'Tis the rich Soil the Conquest doth invite.
> To gather common Stones no labour strives,
> 'Tis for rich Gems the Sun-burnt *Negro* dives.
> Where Plenty springs, or where rich Mines abound,
> The Victory with due Rewards is Crowned;
> To Birds and Beasts is left the *Barren* ground.[24]

The virgin's body promises wealth and fecundity to whomever wins it; conquest and colonization of lands and the exploitation of the earth's resources are compared to courtship: virginity is a commodity on the marriage market. It also suggests that men's plotting is only natural, as the prize is so valuable. As pursuit is inevitable, and innocence insufficient protection, Aaron Hill (1685–1750) warns his subject in his

'Advice to the Virgins, to guard against Flattery' that she must rely on others to keep her on the straight and narrow:

> Propped, on the *parent's* council, and the *friend's*:
> So, leaning *safe*, and wanting space, to *stray*,
> Love's guardian angels crown your nuptial day.

Having successfully resisted the blandishments of unscrupulous hypocrites with the help of family and friends, it is now time for the virgin to thank the author of these cautionary lines: 'Then, *bless* the verse, that from such ruin, saved /An artless conqueror, by success, enslaved'.[25] The virgin in this poem is figured both as powerful ('conqueror') and as vulnerable: victim both to dishonest language ('soft sounds', 'impious falsehood', 'praise', 'flattery') and her own physical urges, which her mind cannot control. The credit for resisting and remaining virginal, therefore, goes not to her but to those who protect her; the virgin is, ultimately, helpless and needs to be shielded from the temptations posed by others and by her own body.

Today, a version of this fear of corruption through art is still present (though in less playful language) in discussions of violent computer games or the impact of nihilistic song lyrics on the psyches of malleable adolescents. As we saw in the last chapter, religious writers continue to warn of the dangers of popular culture in particular. A harsh warning against romance novels is put forward in the eighteenth century by James Fordyce, in his sermon 'On Female Virtue':

> We consider the general run of Novels as utterly unfit for you. Instruction they convey none. They paint scenes of pleasure

and passion altogether improper for you to behold, even with the mind's eye. Their descriptions are often loose and luscious in a high degree; their representations of love between the sexes are almost universally overstrained.

Women were thought to be particularly at risk from these 'loose and luscious' writings, for their emotional and sensual natures could be excited more easily than men's, and were not as tempered by reason. Fordyce makes it clear that the woman who read and enjoyed such literature could not really be considered a virgin at heart, thereby suggesting that reading novels and having sex were part of the same unstoppable trajectory towards ruination:

> What shall we say of certain books, which we are assured (for we have not read them) are in their nature so shameful, in their tendency so pestiferous, and contain such rank treason against the royalty of Virtue, such horrible violation of all decorum, that she who can bear to peruse them must in her soul be a prostitute, let her reputation in life be what it will.

He asks his readers whether they can honestly believe that a 'young woman, pretending to decency' could even 'for a moment [endure] to look on this infernal brood of futility and lewdness'.[26] What we have here are two themes that emerge time and time again, and exist in tension with one another: the innocence of the virgin, which makes her vulnerable, and the suspected artfulness of the virgin who, like all women, is associated with deception and dissimulation.

How to read virginity

In literature, virginity is frequently associated with purity and truthfulness. Influenced by generations of Christian thinking and writings, the connections between light, truth and purity consistently recur. The virgin is frequently compared to the coming of light – the dawn, in particular, but also to the whiteness of snow, the sparkle of jewels, the glistening of stars, the glow of the moon. In Nahum Tate's poem, 'The Virgin', for instance, we are told that she is 'earlier' and 'fairer' than Aurora, the dawn, and that 'the Morning's far less innocent or bright' than she is.[27] Because virginity is aligned with prelapsarian wholeness and innocence, it comes to stand for truth.[28] The virgin does not dissimulate: unlike other women she can be trusted, for her heart and motives are as yet untouched by sinfulness and duplicity. Virginity is also 'natural', in that the virgin is believed to be free from the artifice that comes with experience and is opposed to truth.

This is a recurring theme in contemporary romance novels whose protagonists are virgins. The men they encounter are not only unbelievably wealthy and successful, they are also world-weary and cynical about women. The heroine's virginity unsettles the hero's assumptions that all women are gold-diggers; she is different from them and so offers the possibility of redemption for the lonely, disappointed – and sexually experienced – man. In *The Sheikh's Virgin*, for instance, we are told that Keira 'couldn't give [Kalen] practiced moves, couldn't give him worldly sophistication'; as an innocent she can only give what is presented as 'the truth': 'She could only give him her. Give him her heart, her love, her loyalty'.[29] She is the 'real' goods, representing authenticity as opposed to the artifice of 'practiced moves', which, presumably, is what all those other women gave him instead. Virginity's redemptive potential as presented here is related to the religious view that associated virginity with purity and love. In 'The Three Maries' (1865), for instance, A. J. H. Duganne concludes that Mary Magdalen, the 'Redeemed', '[t]hrough love divine rebears virginity'.[30] In a similar vein, Digby Mackworth Dolben's 'Pro Castitate' (1915) implores Jesus, 'Virgin born of Virgin', to grant him 'Perfect Chastity', above 'Wisdom, power and beauty' – for this would be a gift of 'Love and love and love'.[31] Through their redemptive potential, virgins also bear the promise of transformation – of the possibility of a change of heart and a change of life. This view lives on in an otherwise secular culture and in secular narratives.

In the recent romance novel *Virgin for Sale*, the truth that virginity represents is presented as so exceptional in a corrupted world that it baffles the hero. Constantino Zagorakis is drawn to Lisa Bond, a successful businesswoman in her own right, but sexually inexperienced:

> Why were Lisa's signals so misleading? Her behaviour puzzled him, and he didn't like puzzles. She was acting like a kid, a virgin, even, rather than the ball-breaking bitch everyone said she was.[32]

The 'puzzle' that Lisa represents is indebted to a long tradition of Western thought that associated women not just with the page, but also with mystery. In the Middle Ages, for instance, the truth of a text was described as hidden from view, as 'veiled'. The symbol of the veil, in turn, had 'long been associated with the feminine, rather ambiguously as a sign of both chastity *and* seduction'.[33] This meant that woman (and the virgin in particular) was a mystery, and as such could represent both light *and* darkness, truth *and* danger.

Reading texts and reading women both therefore poses similar challenges to the reader who wants to find out what their 'truth' is. And the truth was found, medieval theorists believed, by penetrating the text, by 'strip[ping] aside the veil of rhetorical ornament to penetrate to a deeper meaning'.[34] Equally, it was thought that the 'truth' of virginity could only really be known at the moment of its loss, when the virgin was penetrated by a man. As John Clare (1793–1864) puts it: 'Soon as touched 'tis gone for ever'.[35] This is particularly problematic in the case of the virgin, for the virgin might be the innocent young woman without experience, but she is also part of fallen humanity and will therefore inevitably be flawed and open to sin, doubly so because she is female. While virginity protects her from her gender's worst flaws, there is always the chance that she will develop them fully, or, indeed, already harbours them in her heart, as John Fordyce fears. Moreover, the idea that sexuality is a natural and healthy part of human nature does not fundamentally ameliorate this anxiety, for woman's sexuality – when and how, how often and with whom she expresses it – always remains a matter for concern.

The simultaneous innocence and nubility of the virgin is a motif that is found in many literary genres from all periods. The number of porn websites obsessed with virgins suggests that this is not about to change. The concepts of whore and virgin turn out to be two sides of the same coin. They don't make sense without each other, and a virgin is certainly always under suspicion of turning into a whore – or already being one, if only in her thoughts. This is less an opposition and more of a sliding scale.

The combination of virginal innocence and budding sexuality is represented as irresistible, offering, as it does, both 'truth' and titillation. Hence, in *The Disobedient Virgin*, Caterina's inexperience simultaneously offers the promise of passion to the man who knows how to awaken it: 'Eyes the color of dark coffee, a mouth that was rosy-pink and generous, innocent of make-up. Innocent, too, he was certain, of a man's taste . . . She was a woman, a gorgeous woman, untouched, unawakened, unexplored.' Wearing 'the garment of a child' over 'the body of a woman', Caterina is both green and ripe; unaware of her own sexuality but ready for the picking.[36] She is utterly natural (free of the deceits of make-up) and artless. The repeated use of adjectives beginning with 'un-' shows that she, like Liesl in *The Sound of Music*, is waiting for a man who will trigger her eruption into full womanhood.

Other texts are far more ambiguous about the relative 'innocence' or 'artfulness' of the virgin, fearing that the former is always on the verge of falling into the latter. After extolling the piousness and purity of the virgin, Tate presents us with a rather more complex set of associations. We are now told about the virgin's pastimes: she 'dissembl[es] Fruits in Wax' and tells stories in the 'artful Webs' of her tapestries, such as that of Ariadne's separation from and loss of Theseus. She excels at these arts: her wax fruits are so lifelike that they 'might even tempt a hungry God to taste' and her tapestries cause the speaker to ask:

> What God inspires our Virgin to express
> Passions that never had to her Heart access?

> For yet she knows not what her Art achieved,
> What 'tis to love, or what to be deceived.[37]

'Art' again can be read to mean both her skill at creating images, and her womanly 'arts': both have the power to seduce. The poem is grappling with the relationship between the virgin, art and knowledge. While the virgin is, by definition, innocent – that is, *unknowing* – her art here depicts emotions that imply a *knowingness*. This virgin artist is not, as in Holmes's poem, a passive, blank page waiting to be inscribed; she *makes* meaning. Yet the creations she brings to life are problematic because they are either brilliant – but false – representations (the astonishingly lifelike wax fruit), or they deal with topics that, should she actually understand them, would compromise her virgin status (passion, love, deception). The uneasy conclusion the speaker arrives at is that she must be inspired by an unknown 'God', which relegates her to a more passive position.

An interest in art or artifice is also shown to be a sign of the onset of dangerous sexuality in previously artless virgins, as Bernard Mandeville's *The Virgin Unmask'd* (1709) suggests. Here we have a series of humorous dialogues between Lucinda, an 'Elderly Maiden Lady', and her nineteen-year-old niece, Antonia. Lucinda is concerned at the change in Antonia, which she dates from the time that Antonia turned fifteen. Whereas they had lived in harmony before this, united in their antipathy towards men, from then on 'The Fashion was all your Discourse; and whatever Money you could get was laid out in Plays and Romances.' Lucinda realizes the change most fully when she observes Antonia being *self-conscious* in front of a man where previously she would have been 'free and

unconcerned'. She describes for Antonia this moment of real-
ization, which occurred when they were passing a stranger in
the street:

> [W]hen he was yet a good Way off I saw you raise your Body,
> and by altering your Gait, assume a certain Firmness in your
> Steps, that was not usual; when he came near, the Stretching
> out of your Neck had pulled up your Bubbies, which were then
> but just Budding out; he looked upon you very hard . . .[38]

While Antonia is still physically a virgin, this new awareness
of her body is portrayed as a loss of innocence, an entry into
a sexualized womanhood, which is repeatedly associated with
artifice. From the dangers of seduction through art, we have
arrived at the dangers of artfulness believed to be inherent in
every woman, even the virgin.

'Female Beauty', by William Kendall, shows the impossible
double bind the female virgin finds herself in, in relation to
knowledge. Kendall begins by comparing virgins to 'vernal
showers, / Sweeter far than opening flowers', and attributes
their beauty to the work of elves and fairies. As one might
expect, virgins are like the morning in their youthfulness, that
'Tranquil hour of artless truth'. Yet here the tone turns threatening:

> But when passion's eager rage
> Sheds th'untimely blight of age;
> When delusive art appears,
> Faithless accents, feigning tears –
> All your blessed protectors fly!
> All your beauties fade and die!

Recalling the narrative of the Fall, the onset of passion brings about the 'blight of age', the replacement of innocence with 'delusive art', the fading of beauty and, ultimately, death. Virginity is aligned with a magical realm in this poem, yet the spell breaks when the 'Lovely looks of innocence' turn to 'Faithless accents, feigning tears'.[39] Virginity is the ultimate ideal of female beauty, yet its demise is inevitable. The virgin cannot prevent this happening to her, because in order to avoid it she would have to know what it was she was meant to avoid; once she knew about that, she would already have forfeited the innocence that makes her so delightful.[40]

The move from chastising unscrupulous male seducers to blaming the virgin for her downfall can be found not just by comparing different narratives, but sometimes within a few lines of the same story or poem. Heyrick, while ostensibly warning virgins of 'plots and stratagems' concocted by besotted lovers, quickly locates the blame and responsibility in the virgin herself:

> Guard then your Beauty; 'tis a Dangerous Store,
> A Fatal Treasure, that hath Ruined more,
> Than ever were Wretched made by being poor.

As it is not clear who has been ruined, one can assume that the virgin is responsible both for her own well-being *and* that of her admirers, as they are vulnerable to her 'fatal treasure'. What starts out as advice to the virgin ends up by being a warning to her: 'You're *Angels*, while You do admit no Stain; / But when You fall, You *Mortals* are again'. That we get from heavenly innocence to intimations of the Fall within thirty-five lines in Heyrick's poem reveals the assumptions underlying such well-meant tones: ultimately, the virgin is somehow to

A nineteenth-century engraving entitled *Approaching Ruin*, in which a young man is stealing the clothes of a young bather who is in a state of semi-undress. The title presumably refers to the ruin of her reputation through his act.

blame for the desire she arouses in others. Were she behaving modestly, chastely, this would not happen:

> *Be Virtuous and be thought so*; Few there be,
> That dare attempt upon Your Chastity,
> If no unwary Action did precede,
> By which they gathered hopes, they might Succeed.[41]

It is a more articulate – if not more sophisticated – version of 'she was asking for it'. It also means that a virgin is always suspected of colluding in her deflowering, irrespective of the context that might happen in.

An earlier example of this view – and perhaps more chilling, because it spells out the consequences – is found in Chaucer's 'The Physician's Tale'. When we are introduced to the fourteen-year-old Virginia, we are told not only of her astonishing beauty, but also of her impeccable virginity, which is both physical and spiritual: 'As well in soul as body chaste was she'. We are assured that she has no falseness ('No counterfeited expressions had she'): Virginia is the real thing. The praise of her virtues goes on for many lines – she is held up as a model for other maidens to imitate, a paragon of virginal perfection. However, despite this hyperbole – and despite the fact that it is made clear that no sin or lechery inhabit her – she is the one who has to bear the consequences of the judge Apius's illicit desire for her. When Virginia's father is made aware of Apius's designs on his daughter, he tells her that there are only two options for her: death or shame. After swooning, she is quick to see the positive side: 'Blessed be God that I shall die a maiden! / Give me my death, before I am disgraced.' Her father obliges, cutting off her head with his sword. Afterwards he forgives Apius's trespass with the same alacrity that he showed in killing his daughter.[42]

Although Virginia has complied completely with the ideal of virginity, she is punished for Apius's desire; as she is a symbol of her father's honour, death is better than loss of virginity and the shame that follows it. One critic points out that none of this would have happened if Virginia had not been seen by Apius.[43] Implicit in this view is the idea that if a man desires a woman, she cannot be truly innocent; that there is something in her that inflames his desire and that she is therefore also to blame for the consequences. No matter how obedient – how 'pure' – the woman is, she is at fault if illicit male desire focuses on her. She should have been *more* invisible, *more* absent. Even when the virgin is recognized to be utterly blameless – as in the virgin martyr legends – she must still die in order to demonstrate her faith and, one suspects, to place her maintained virginity beyond doubt.

A woman's reputation – how she is seen by those around her – is crucial to successfully maintained virginity. A blow to her reputation is the first step in what then becomes an unstoppable slide towards loss of virginity, physical virtue and social respect. Rumours are started by some flaw in the virgin herself; the logic involved dictates that there can be no smoke without fire. In *The V Club*, a recent book by Kate Brian aimed at a female teen readership, the lives of several friends are followed in their final school year as they compete for a scholarship award that demands 'purity' as one of its conditions. They set up the 'V[irgin] Club', and the different attitudes of each of the young women to purity are what motivates the plot, from Eva, the 'purest of the pure', to her best friend Debbie, the 'kissing slut'. As these two compete for the affections of the only male member of the V Club, the virginal and rather smug Riley, their other friends try to understand their own lives in the light of maintained virginity – even Kai, the one member who is no longer a virgin due to the blandishments of the seductive (and foreign) Andres.

Debbie, the most flirtatious of them all (though still a virgin), grapples mainly with what she fears are the rumours circulating in the school about her promiscuity. Whereas she starts off with a devil-may-care attitude, her crush on Riley leads her to rethink her image. As concerns about her reputation preoccupy her, she begins to judge herself according to how she thinks others see her, especially Riley ('He thinks you're a whore', 'Riley thinks I'm dirty, just like the rest of the world does'): 'If she wanted him to like her, she was going to have to refute all those rumours – somehow . . . She had to make him forget everything he'd heard about her. She had to make him realise she was not the slut of the century.'

In contrast, Eva – who eventually gets the guy – conveys her inner purity through outer signs, for instance a lack of vanity and reluctance to participate in activities portrayed as typical of emerging female sexuality: 'Her clothes were baggy and her hair was in bad need of a brushing . . . She didn't do parties. She didn't do flirting. She didn't do dressing up for guys.' In the end, Debbie proves to herself and to the world that she is not a 'slut' in a public demonstration which relies on physical evidence. When she overhears someone saying about her 'God, she's such a slut' at a party, she confronts the full room with the question, 'What makes you all think I've had so much sex?'[44] It turns out that their knowledge is based on rumour and on the empty boasts boys have made. When she asks those in the room who present has had sex with her, several of them raise their hands. This is when she springs her trap, asking whether they can tell her what tattoo she has on her hip. After some uncertainty, they guess that it is a heart. In a spirited flourish she slowly unbuttons her skirt, teasing her audience and finally reveals . . . a honeybee.

While this is portrayed as a triumphant and redemptive moment for Debbie, it assumes that women are judged according to their sexual behaviour. Had she had sex – either with just one or with all of the 'guys' present – and had they been able to guess her tattoo, she would have confirmed her reputation as a 'slut'. The possibility that someone might have seen a tattoo on her hip while *not* having sex with her lingers in the background. The fragility of Debbie's status is clear; it is akin to a situation that might take place in a courtroom. A woman's sexuality is not her own – and her social identity is dependent on the stories that others tell about her, true or false.

This is not surprising, given that in the Middle Ages even the Virgin Mary was not considered exempt from the dangers of a damaged reputation. In one fifteenth-century manuscript, we find a series of pageants that dramatize her life, several of which focus on allegations that the Virgin Mary is not virginal at all. Virgin, mother and wife as well as more than human through her own miraculous birth, Mary cannot be read according to traditional notions of 'nature' or comfortably confined to any of the categories that Western medieval – and modern – society reserves for women. Because of the nature of drama, the ambiguity of the virginal identity can be represented in a highly visible and physical way. It also shows that just *being* a virgin is never enough; only seeing is believing. Although Mary is shown in these plays to behave according to the ideals set out by her husband and by the religious authorities, she still falls foul of public perception. Consequently, she is unjustly accused of sexual misconduct – and of lying – three times: by Joseph in *Joseph's Doubt*, by the community and courts in *The Trial*, and by the midwife in *The Nativity*.[45]

While Joseph knows of his wife's vow of chastity, he finds her pregnant body frightening and, interpreting it as a sign of her infidelity, fears that he has been 'betrayed'. Much of the humour that is undoubtedly present throughout this episode is derived from the fact that Joseph, who is represented as an old man, understandably scoffs at the story that his young, beautiful wife tells him, which is that an angel came to her in his absence and that her pregnancy is the result of a miracle. A

This late fifteenth-century painting by the Master of Marienleben depicts the birth of the Virgin Mary, which is imagined within a contemporary late-medieval context.

likely story, is his response. Just as Joseph reads her womb, which is 'swollen' and stands out prominently, as evidence of sexual trespass, her accusers in *The Trial* refer to her pregnant body as the prime 'witness' in their case against her. In *The Nativity*, the expertise of the midwives (which reflects another form of 'common knowledge') is rattled when their considerable professional experience, which leads them to say that a woman cannot bear a child without experiencing pain, is proven wrong. Each time, heaven intervenes to clear her name: Joseph is told by an angel that Mary is as virginal as she was when he married her; in *The Trial* a magic potion absolves her; in *The Nativity*, the midwife Salomé's hand withers 'dead and dry as clay' in punishment for her disbelief after she takes up Mary's offer to examine her genitalia for signs of virginity.

In each instance, it is not Mary's perfect conformity with the ideals of chaste female behaviour that refutes her doubters, but divine intervention, which does not bode well for the woman who does not have such aid in clearing her name. It is her outward appearance which her detractors and doubters seek to confirm; the disguise, in their eyes, lies in her claim to virginity. Of course her body, especially when pregnant, *does* appear to contradict what she says, but there is a more fundamental anxiety underlying these stories. Virginity and promiscuity, though presented as polar opposites, are actually similar: both are perceived as difficult to control and are therefore potentially disorderly and threatening. The fear of the woman who pretends to be something she is not is found in many medieval 'chronicles, poems [and] saints' lives', which related 'attempts to unmask women, to subject them to tests, and to expose them for what they really were'.[46] In the case of virgin martyrs, for example, virginal integrity is 'proven' in countless narratives through the torture and dismemberment of the virgin body. In fact, much of this material focuses on women whose main aim is to maintain their intactness. Chastity and virginity caused anxiety almost more than any other female identity because they were always subject to doubt: 'Behind the veil of modesty lurked the specter of insatiable female sexual appetite.'[47]

It is important to emphasize that the pageants that dramatize the testing of Mary's virginity are not critical of a society that judges women's worth according to their sexual behaviour – after all, the mother of God is exceptional, and her exceptionality only highlights the failings of other women. What they do show is that reading virginity is problematic, and that it needs to be proven repeatedly because a woman's reputation is both fragile and absolutely central to her social status. Reputation was taken very seriously in medieval society and court records show that women suffered disproportionately from sexual defamation.[48] A woman's sexual reputation is still considered important to how she is judged by those around her, be it family, peer group or even law court. In this sense one could say that Debbie's test in *The V Club* is really a testing *of* Debbie – a modern version of the chastity tests that occur in literature from at least the fifth century BC onwards. In medieval writings – romance, saint's life or even history – there are numerous examples in which a woman is tested in order to reveal whether she is truly a virgin (or a chaste wife) or not. This can take the form of drinking from a goblet, which spills on those who are unchaste, to walking on red-hot ploughshares without sustaining injury, as Queen Emma, Edward the Confessor's mother, is said to have done to prove that she was innocent of the charge of adultery.[49] Two of the most well-known examples, taken from history and literature respectively, are that of Joan of Arc, whose virginity was tested numerous times, and that of the legendary virgin whose purity could tame the wild and magical unicorn.[50] In all of these, the 'truth' of the virgin's body is proven by some miraculous – and highly visible – public event.

Reputation works differently for men. As Telly, the gawky adolescent protagonist of the controversial film *Kids* (dir. Larry Clark, 1995) explains to his friend Casper: 'If you deflower a girl, man, aw, you're the man, no one can ever do that again, you know?' Casper agrees and suggests that it confers a fame that goes beyond death, for all those deflowered virgins would remember the person they lost their virginity to. In this way, a man can create a reputation for himself in this life as well as beyond, at the risk of the woman losing hers.[51]

If chastity tests are meant to provide clear evidence of a woman's sexual status, they are often shown to be anything but foolproof. In Thomas Middleton and William Rowley's seventeenth-century play *The Changeling*, for example, Alsemero, who is about to marry Beatrice, wants to test her virginity with a potion. She, however, has lost her virginity to the wicked De Flores, in return for his murder of her fiancé, Alonzo, whom she wants removed once she meets Alsemero. When she realizes that her maidenhead is the only payment De Flores will accept, she is devastated. He, however, points out to her that her change of affection from Alonzo to Alsemero itself suggests that she is not as constant as one might expect from a true virgin. He draws an unbroken line from her feelings to her actions, telling her that she shouldn't be so apprehensive of losing her physical virginity, as her inner lack of continence proves her to be a slut already: 'Though thou writ'st a maid [*would call yourself a virgin*], thou whore in thy affection! / 'Twas changed from thy first love, and that's a kind / Of whoredom in thy heart'. Fearing for her life, Beatrice breaks into Alsemero's medical closet and reads about the symptoms that a true virgin is meant to exhibit after drinking the potion. As a result, she passes as a virgin. For the moment, her performance is completely successful, and Alsemero, delighted, embraces her, exclaiming that she is 'Chaste as the breath of heaven, or morning's womb, / That brings the day forth'.[52]

Defloration

Despite the recognition that there is no single, absolute way of ascertaining maintained virginity, either through behaviour or through physical examination, many texts rely on the pain and bleeding caused by penetration as signs of lost virginity. In the medieval *The Romance of the Rose*, the narrator finally gains his heart's desire and is allowed to 'pluck' the rosebud. Even though he has promised 'to do nothing violent', it is represented as unavoidable:

> [W]hen I could not immediately break the barrier, I struggled so hard and with such violence that I was drenched in sweat . . . However, I continued with my assault until I noticed a narrow passage . . . Nothing . . . could have prevented me from sliding my staff all the way in . . . I found the passage to me very narrow, and it was quite impossible for me to pass that way. Indeed, if I understood the nature of that path correctly,

no one had ever passed that way, for I was the first to do so, and the place was not yet in the habit of collecting tolls.[53]

The levels of violence accompanying defloration may differ, depending on context or genre, but pain and blood are required nonetheless. Judy Blume's novel *Forever* (1975), praised for its sensitive portrayal of teen sexuality, draws on the signs of tightness, pain and blood to signal Katherine's lost virginity. Here, the sex being described is mutual and Katherine's boyfriend Michael is hapless rather than inconsiderate. When Katherine tells him to push harder during their first attempt at sex, he replies: 'I'm trying, Kath . . . but it's very tight in there.' When Michael comes (quite quickly) Katherine feels 'a big thrust, followed by a quick sharp pain', but, to her disappointment, not much else. Though she is surprised to discover that she does not bleed as much as she expected to, there are still the telltale 'drops of blood' to mark the occasion.[54]

John Cleland's erotic novel *Fanny Hill* (1748–9), presented as a memoir of the eponymous protagonist, makes much more of the pain and violence of first intercourse. This is how Fanny describes her loss of virginity:

> [A]pplying the point of his machine to the slit, into which he sought entrance: it was so small, he could scarce assure himself of its being rightly pointed. He looks, he feels, and satisfies himself; then driving on with fury, its prodigious stiffness, thus impacted, wedge-like, breaks the union of those parts, and gained him just the insertion of the tip of it, lip deep; which being sensible of, he improved his advantage, and following well his stroke, in a straight line, forcible deepens his penetration; but

put me to such intolerable pain, from the separation of the sides of that soft passage by a hard thick body, I could have screamed out . . . At length the tender texture of that tract giving way to such fierce tearing and rending, he pierced somewhat further into me: and now, outrageous and no longer his own master, but borne headlong away by the fury and overmettle of that member, now exerting itself with a kind of native rage, he breaks in, carries all before him, and one violent merciless lunge sent it, imbrued and reeking with virgin blood, up to the very hilt in me. Then! then all my resolution deserted me: I screamed out, and fainted away with the sharpness of the pain; and, as he told me afterwards, on his drawing out, when emission was over with him, my thighs were instantly all in a stream of blood that flowed from the wounded torn passage.

Yet even while this description incorporates all of the incontrovertible proofs of virginity to excess, the novel playfully undermines this when Fanny, now sexually experienced, relates how she meets up with a lover who is so well-endowed that he leaves her bleeding again, as if she had lost 'a kind of second maidenhead'.[55]

A rather different understanding of the relationship between virginity and male penetration is offered in Kevin Smith's screenplay to the film *Chasing Amy* (dir. Kevin Smith, 1997). In one scene, the main characters, Holden and Alyssa, have a discussion about what it means to be a virgin. Because Alyssa is a lesbian, Holden insists that she is still a virgin, exposing the heterosexist assumptions that underpin his understanding of virginity. In turn, Alyssa, who keeps questioning his definition, forces him to modify it, thereby showing its arbitrariness. Finally, Holden falls back on the hymen: 'Okay, I'll revise. Virginity is lost when the hymen is broken.' Alyssa tells him that this would mean: 'I lost my virginity at ten, because I fell on a fence post when I was ten, and it broke my hymen', concluding with the quip, 'Now I have to tell people that I lost it to a wooden post I'd known all my whole young life?'[56] Although Holden can accept that Alyssa has slept with many women, once he finds out that he is not the first man she has been with sexually – and, moreover, that she has been in a threesome with two men – he responds with jealous rage, ruining the relationship. Underlying this rage, though it is not fully articulated by Holden, is not just his insecurity because of her greater experience, which he ultimately admits, but also his privileging of male penetration, despite the fact that Alyssa has shattered his illusions about lesbian sex being necessarily non-penetrative. Penetration with a penis remains for him the defining sex act, which means that, despite their discussion, Alyssa is still a virgin for him – a woman untouched by a man. Ultimately, while the scene is funny and effective in its unravelling of stereotypical assumptions of virginity and its challenge to heterosexual expectations, it shows just how persistent and powerful such assumptions are.

Even blood and penetration have their limits as proof, as *Fanny Hill* shows. The possibility of a woman refurnishing herself with the bodily signs of virginity provides the theme for many bawdy ditties and other literary accounts. As 'The Loving Chamber-Maid' (1675) tells us: 'The famous Matrons / Of Wherstone will tell / That they can a Maiden-head / Sixty times sell'.[57] A similar sentiment is expressed in 'The Country Miss New Come in Fashion' (1677), which compares the lusty yet innocent country girls to the diseased and artful city girls: 'Clap she never had like Miss of the Town, / That's painted and patched, and lives up and down'.[58] In *Kids*, Telly explains in the opening sequence why it is that he is obsessed with fucking young girls: 'Virgins. I love 'em. No diseases. No loose-as-a-goose pussy. No skank. No nuthin'. Just pure pleasure.'[59] In an unpleasant film 'comedy' by Jean-Pierre Marois, *Live Virgin* (1999),[60] the market-place value of virginity as consumer product is central to the story in which teenager Katrina, determined to rebel against her porn-film-producer father, decides to lose her virginity live, via the internet and on pay-per-view television. Members of the audience can buy cybernetic suits that allow them to share the experience of her 'deflowerer'.

Virginity, however doubted or 'patched up', is a desirable commodity. Like literature or film, it promises pleasure and can fetch a good price if it tells a convincing story: 'New plays and maidenheads are near akin – / Much followed both, for both much money given, / If they stand sound and well'.[61] Whether the virgin is aristocratic, bourgeois, or a working girl, a bride or a prostitute, her virginity is presented as her most precious asset on the market. The prostituted or seduced virgin commands a higher price, not least because she is free of disease, and the virgin bride ensures the uncontaminated continuity of the man's family line, as well as potentially allowing her father to participate in some social climbing. Therefore, as Prospero puts it in *The Tempest*, when he tells Ferdinand that he has his permission to marry his daughter Miranda: '[A]s my gift and thine own acquisition / Worthily purchased, take my daughter'.[62]

Independent virgins

An alternative to this view of virginity-as-commodity to be disposed of by – or exchanged between – men is found in some writings on virginity, mainly by women, in which virginity allows them to escape the demands imposed by a male-dominated society. Frequently, this is also linked to the idea that virginity becomes the primary and positive precondition for women's writing. Written in the seventeenth century, Jane Barker's 'A Virgin Life' opens by addressing the 'Powers' that have 'bestowed on me / So great a kindness for Virginity'. She begs them to help her escape 'Mens almost Omnipotent Amours'. For the speaker in this poem, virginity is not about innocence and lack of self-awareness; in fact, it is precisely the opposite. In contrast to those who enter marriage ('Like harmless Kids, that are pursued by Men, / For safety run into a Lion's Den'), she has the strength to stay true to her virginal life, which she equates with virtue, friendship, being a good subject and a good Christian. Her life is dedicated to 'serve her God, enjoy her Books and Friends' – an explicit alignment of maintained virginity and the attainment of knowledge.[63]

'Knowledge' here means something quite different from the way it is used by many male writers on virginity, who equate it automatically with sexual knowledge, or a woman's awareness of herself as sexual being. In contrast, Barker equates knowledge with intellectual knowledge, which in the period she wrote was still very much perceived as a male prerogative. Book knowledge was, as I have shown in other chapters, considered too abstract, too spiritual and rational for women, who were thought to be governed by their physical, sensual natures. Yet the speaker here is making precisely the argument that remaining a virgin allows a woman to escape the demands of the body – of sex in marriage, of pregnancy and childbirth – giving her the room and time to think, read and, presumably, write.

Also in the seventeenth century, Margaret Cavendish tells the story of Lady Happy in her *Convent of Pleasure*. Having inherited much wealth from her recently deceased father, Lady Happy decides not to marry but to create a community for 'many Noble Persons of my own Sex' who are of her social class and 'are resolved to live a single life, and vow Virginity'. Yet hers will not be a religious community: 'My Cloister shall not be a Cloister of restraint, but a place for freedom, not to vex the Senses but to please them.' This 'convent' is served only by female attendants, which means that there are 'Women-Physicians, Surgeons and Apothecaries'; in short, there are 'Women for every Office and Employment', placing women in roles that they were barred from in reality.[64] The benefits that such a 'convent' provides are made clear in Lady Happy's speech on the trials and tribulations of a young wife:

> Put the case I should Marry the best of Men, if any best there be; yet would a Married life have more crosses and sorrows then pleasure, freedom, or happiness; nay Marriage to those that are virtuous is a greater restraint than a Monastery ... And since there is so much folly, vanity and falsehood in Men, why should Women trouble and vex themselves for their sake; for retiredness bars the life from nothing else but Men.[65]

One later view of virginity – as empowering personal choice – is related to this earlier argument that it allows women to live a life not determined by male expectations, especially concerning sex. As Mandy says to her fellow-members of the V Club, 'If you're a member of this club, you're clearly embracing your choice not to have sex.'[66] 'Freedom' from sex is presented as allowing the woman to engage in activities otherwise barred to her, such as intellectual pursuits, or, in more recent writings, the pursuit of a university education, career or self-realization.

In Chaucer's 'The Knight's Tale', the young virgin Emily prays to the goddess Diana to be allowed to remain a virgin, describing the freedoms it gives her:

> 'I am, as you know, still one of your fellowship,
> A maiden, and [I] love hunting,
> And to walk in the woods so wild,
> And not to be a wife, with child.'[67]

Similar imagery is used in 'The Monk's Tale' to describe the queen Zenobia, who was '[s]o worthy ... in arms and so fierce' that from childhood on she 'fled the duties of women'. Instead, she spent her time hunting ferocious beasts, such as 'lions, leopards, and bears', in the woods and running through the mountains at night. She is so strong and hardy that she can wrestle with any young man, and the Monk concludes by telling us: 'She kept her virginity from everyone; / She would be shackled to no man'.[68] Both Emily and Zenobia are described as martial in their maidenhood, engaging in activities that are clearly opposed to the 'duties of women'.

As one critic points out, in the Middle Ages and beyond, '[i]n a very general sense, the body of any military woman was an Amazon body'.[69] Thought to live in the barbaric region of Scythia, to the north of the Black Sea, these legendary women were famous for being fearsome warriors. In his fourteenth-century travel narrative, which was wildly popular in its own time and in following centuries, John Mandeville describes the home of the Amazons thus:

Next to Chaldea is the land of Amazoun, which we call the Maiden Land or the Land of Women; no man lives there, only women. This is not because, as some say, no man can live there, but because the women will not allow men to rule the kingdom.[70]

Due to their exotic appeal, Amazons were popular figures in medieval and later literary productions. In her *Book of the City of Ladies* (1405), the French writer Christine de Pizan uses the Amazons as an example of admirable femininity in her quest to defend women against the 'many wicked insults' that men write about them. Each example she gives is, she says, a building block out of which the beautiful City of Ladies will be constructed; that of the Amazons is among the first to be enlisted in the creation of the city's foundations. Christine takes pains to highlight these

A thirteenth-century miniature showing Penthesilea, Queen of the Amazons, leading her warriors into battle against Achilles and the Greeks.

female warriors' virtue as well as their valour, prudence and discipline. Some of them, she says, choose to remain virgins, like Synoppe, who has 'such a great and lofty heart that not for a day in her life did she deign to couple with a man'.[71]

All-female communities and martial maidens were not just praised, however, for the very qualities that made them admirable also threatened the long-held assumption that women needed to belong to some man, be he father, husband or lover. Thus, while these women are praised for their man-like courage on the one hand, that also marks them as potentially problematic and threatening. Women who withdrew from the heterosexual arena, or challenged its hierarchical assumptions, became the target for accusations of 'unfeminine' and 'unnatural' behaviour – views which live on in the caricature of the butch, man-hating feminist. A nineteenth-century version of this is found in Henry Ellison's 'Epicoene, or Strong-Minded Women'. Raging against those who fight for women's rights, Ellison claims that these are 'the "foolish virgins"', 'clamouring ... for their "rights"', with 'tongues far better furnished than their brains'. They have not experienced, or do not appreciate, 'the consecrate delights / Of holy unions' and therefore 'their unblessed veins' are not flowing with 'Maternal blood'. He reminds them of their *real* rights with stern contempt:

> Vain babblers! rights you have;
> And *duties*. Yours to educate mankind;
> To make it pious, pure, self-scorning, brave;
> To give speech to the dumb, sight to the blind!
> Teach the child right – that right God Himself gave –
> And woman, *righted*, in the man the child will find![72]

What Ellison implies here is that even women who have had the fortunate experience of conjugal sex are 'foolish virgins' if they demand political rights, because they have not seen the true calling of womankind, or understood the true meaning of 'rights' when applied to women.

While lifelong virginity had a place in Catholic ideology, the emphasis on marriage as the natural human condition by Protestantism added fuel to the disparagement of female communities. This sentiment is expressed clearly in Andrew Marvell's 'Upon Appleton House', in which a critique of Catholicism is expressed alongside the notion that it unjustly challenges patriarchal prerogative, seducing young women away from their proper roles and duties as brides and wives into a falsely utopian sisterhood. The nuns lure away the bride-to-be, convincing her to join their community by outlining its delights and freedoms. The 'subtle nuns' see themselves as 'virgin amazons', promised 'brighter Robes and Crowns of Gold' in the afterlife. Marvell calls them 'hypocrite witches', accusing them of hidden, vicious vices. In the end, the groom succeeds in brushing the nuns away 'like Flies', and triumphantly reclaims the weeping bride as his own.[73] Similarly, in *The Canterbury Tales*, Emily and Zenobia end up marrying – urged on by the gods, male leaders and friends. In *The Convent of Pleasure*, Lady Happy falls in love with one of her fellow-virgins only to discover that 'she' is, in fact, a 'he' in disguise: she marries him. Marriage shows the freedoms of the virginal life to be limited, and safely relocates the women in the domestic, marital sphere that puts an end to all such waywardness.

The contrasting interpretations of martial virginity are perhaps nowhere starker than in the example of Joan of Arc. The sheer number of literary and cinematic productions that have been based on her life since her execution in the fifteenth century is evidence of the warrior-maiden's power to fascinate, demonstrating how virginity motivates plot lines. No other female figure – aside from, perhaps, Elizabeth I – has been read and interpreted and re-written so many times, and in such different ways: Joan the inspired virgin martyr; Joan the patriot; Joan the hysteric; Joan the deluded fanatic; Joan the feminist; Joan the lesbian.[74]

Calling herself 'la Pucelle', Joan announced herself and was believed by her supporters to be a pure virgin, the sign that God was on her side and leading her to victory.[75] For her detractors, she was an unnatural woman: some suspected her of not being a woman at all. When Joan was brought to trial in Rouen by the English and the Burgundians in 1431, the accusation levelled against her was that of heresy. Her 'heresy' consisted in obeying the saintly voices that she said spoke to her, rather than the authority of the Catholic Church. This disobedience was made visible – with fatal consequences – when she resumed wearing the male clothes that had been forbidden her, saying that her voices had told her to do so.[76] The contradictory interpretations of Joan's cross-dressing in this period show how what signalled holy femininity to some could be read as monstrous femininity by others. Her supporters drew on a tradition of holy women – holy virgins in particular – who had cross-dressed in order to save their people or to escape worldly obligations in their longing for a spiritual life.[77] Her detractors, in turn, drew on the works of theologians who had condemned or forbidden cross-dressing, stating that it promoted licentiousness, or that it was an abomination because it challenged the natural order created by God. Then history and literature conspired to undermine the virgin status that lent credence to her ambitions. Before her trial, Joan's virginity had been subjected to physical examination numerous times, both by her supporters and her enemies. All concluded that she was indeed a virgin. Yet from the fifteenth century on, English accounts began to suggest that she wasn't – insinuating that her cross-dressing allowed

This photographic image presents itself as a portrait of Joan of Arc and is clearly concerned to combine Joan's martial qualities with purity and femininity. While it depicts her in gleaming armour, this only highlights the delicate fragility of the model, with her long, wavy hair, large eyes and childlike features.

her to engage in illicit sexual activity, making her appear monstrous rather than saintly.

One of the best-known literary examples of this is found in Shakespeare's *Henry VI, Part I*, which shows Joan relying on the help of demons and presents her as unnatural in her denial of proper male authority.[78] Taken by the English to see her father, her heated denial of his paternity shows her to be a rebellious and wilful daughter; her rejection of him is represented as another version of her rejection of the 'proper' masculine rule of the English (for the French dauphin is depicted as effeminate and useless). Joan's words paint a picture of her virginity as a fantasy that she has concocted, part of a wishful and wilful self-fashioning that denies the limitations of her birth, her social class and her sex:

> First, let me tell you whom you have condemned:
> Not me begotten of a shepherd swain,
> But issued from the progeny of kings;
> Virtuous and holy; chosen from above,
> By inspiration of celestial grace,
> To work exceeding miracles on earth.
> [. . .]
>   Joan of Arc hath been
> A virgin from her tender infancy,
> Chaste and immaculate in very thought;
> Whose maiden blood, thus rigorously effused,
> Will cry for vengeance at the gates of heaven.[79]

It is also shown to be an empty boast. Not only have we seen her offer her body to the demons in exchange for their help, but, when she realizes after this speech that the English will condemn her, she announces that she is pregnant in order to defer her execution. When she is asked who the father might be, she ties herself in knots, listing a number of possible contenders. The English mock her ('the holy maid with child!'), showing her to be not a virgin but a whore: 'Strumpet, thy words condemn thy brat and thee.' This theme is already evident in the first act, when Talbot refers to Joan as 'pucelle or puzzel', meaning 'virgin or harlot'.[80]

Unnatural, unfashionable, uncanny

The argument that sex was a natural human function was, as *The Romance of the Rose* shows, already made by medieval writers. As the Wife of Bath says, genitals were made by God for a reason and she will not hold back from using them: 'In marriage I will use my instrument / As freely as my Maker has given it.'[81] The epithalamium, a song celebrating marriage, takes the approach that virginity is a prerequisite for marriage, but that it is not a condition that should be prolonged or maintained for its own sake. The wedding is a threshold, a transition from innocence to sexual initiation. This is celebrated with particular vigour by Thomas d'Urfey in his 'An Epithalamium Sung at the Marriage of Lady W–':

> What is a Maidenhead? ah what?
> Of which weak fools so often prate?
> 'Tis the young Virgins pride and boast,
> Yet never was found but when 'twas lost[.][82]

Virginity can be dismissed lightly in such a context. The hypocrisy here is that it could nonetheless only be relinquished in a very specific and regulated context if the woman wanted to maintain the reputation that was so important to her social survival. This approach associated virginity with life because virgins are thought of as girls on the brink of womanhood – ripening and fertile, ready to copulate and procreate. They are both young (distant from death) and innocent (distant from illness, both physical and spiritual), yet have full sexual potential. Virginity here is valued, but mainly for the promise it holds out for future pleasure and productivity within the socially sanctioned institution of heterosexual marriage.

Similarly, in contemporary romance novels with virgin heroines, the women portrayed are certainly not asexual and they are not condemned for being sexual creatures. What *is* nonetheless also emphasized is that this 'natural' sexuality needs to be awoken, and that, in turn, can only happen with the 'right' man; thus, these virgins manage to be both innocent *and* sexy ('She'd gone from innocent virgin to tempting vixen in a heartbeat, and he was crazy about both of them'[83]). While they are highly sexualized and highly sexed, they don't 'sleep around'; they are uninhibited and capable of pleasure and abandon with one man only, and the sign of the specialness of their 'gift' to this man is that he recognizes it: 'As silken tissue stretched around him, an incontrovertible truth assailed him. Nothing but marriage would do.'[84] In novels such as *The V Club* or Louise Harwood's *Six Reasons to Stay a Virgin*, those who take up the position of virginity defend it to their peers by saying that it is a gift, to be given to that one special person. As one protagonist explains wistfully, 'I can't help thinking what a lovely thing it would be, *for me* . . . to give my virginity to the right man'.[85] Similarly Riley, the only male virgin in *The V Club*, tells Eva: '[W]hat better gift can you give the person you're gonna spend the rest of your life with . . .?'[86] The contrast between his outlook – portrayed as both less masculine (in the eyes of his male peers) and *more* masculine (in the logic of the narrative) – and that of the other boys is what makes him so attractive to many of the girls. While these texts frequently comment on how virginity is considered an outdated – even 'archaic' – value, they conclude by showing that it remains an important one, to be handled with care. On the other hand, none of them considers that maintained virginity is either unproblematic or desirable – it then becomes a symptom of neurosis, a lamentable fear of life.

Despite the common view that virginity was valued until the sexual revolution of the 1960s, when it became something to be embarrassed about, literary sources show that a portrayal of virginity as dull goes back much further. While there is a difference between the view that virginity is unnatural and unhealthy, and the view that it is inherently unimportant or outmoded, the two are also interconnected. There is literary evidence of this from as early as the seventeenth century. Barker, for instance, protests against such a denigration of virginity in 'A Virgin Life': '[I]n this happy Life let me remain, / Fearless of Twenty five and all its train, / Of slights or scorns, or being called Old Maid, / Those Goblins which so many have betrayed'.[87] Others speculate that virginity is not in fact valued for itself, but maintained mainly because of lack of opportunity. Thus Aston Cokain, in 'Of Galla' (1658): 'Galla still hath her maidenhead; And why? / She is unhandsome, and her price too high.'[88]

For 'Ephelia' the maidenhead is a troublesome trinket, a 'fantastic Ill' and 'loathed Disease', something that nobody loves and everyone wants to get rid of. Women who obey the injunction to remain virginal are 'Ill-natured, Ugly, Peevish, Proud' and do so only because they lack the 'Power to Rebel'.[89] For John Cunningham (1729–63), in 'A Man to My Mind', it is a question of fashion: the maiden must find a suitable husband now that 'wedlock's in vogue, and stale virgins despised'.[90] Cowley (1618–67) calls it the 'worst Estate even of the sex that's worst', nothing but 'a point Imaginary', a 'thing of subtle, slippery kind, / Which Women lose, and yet no Man can find'.[91] In his 'Spirits of distress, of every occupation', Charles Dibdin (1745–1814) echoes this view, defining the lifelong virgin purely in terms of her perceived barrenness, and adjuring her to appear to him alongside the spirits of deceived Quakers, foolish old men and reluctant hypocrites: 'Spirit of a virgin, old and antiquated, / Who forty long winters have sighed out unmated'.[92] The tone is unmistakably one of derision; what use does the ageing virgin have now that she is old and, like winter, frigid and barren? Worth nothing in and of herself, she can only sigh and wait for the death that she has come to embody.

The difference with twentieth-century versions of this approach is that virginity additionally becomes associated with dull domesticity, a sign of oppressive social expectations and a submission to bourgeois mediocrity: 'Cabbages no doubt are virgins / Growing plump behind the wire netting / In each suburban garden, waiting for / The slug to climb and rape them'. These are like the virgin who 'opens to her man's prick / (Only after the proper contract) / In a motel, or a caravan',[93] reducing sex to a legal exchange: sex for respectability, a kind of socially sanctioned prostitution, but less honest. James Broughton's Don Giovanni concludes that he is not made for 'minuets Goody-Two-Shoed and petite', preferring 'more bitter sweets' to 'purity that bores', asking laconically: 'Is there something dull about the innocent? /That your simple glowing is a glow too pure, and an irritant?'[94]

The notion that virginity is good and natural, but only if it is lived as a phase preceding marriage (or a serious monogamous relationship) is perhaps most clearly articulated in those writings that claim that, if maintained for too long, it can result in illness or even be likened to a living death. Robert Burton, for instance, echoes (though in a different tone) the views of Genius in *The Romance of the Rose* several centuries later, when he proclaims in his *Anatomy of Melancholy* (1621) that vowed virginity is 'against the laws of nature'. Joining monastic orders, he writes, causes a desperate battle to rage within the individual who has thus dedicated him- or herself to a single life: 'Nature, youth, and his furious passion forcibly inclines, and rageth on the one side; but their order and vow checks them on the other'. This battle can only lead to disaster, both on a personal level and for society as a whole:

> I am sure, from such rash vows and inhuman manner of life proceed many inconveniences, many diseases, many vices, masturbation, satyriasis, priapismus, melancholy, madness, fornication, adultery, buggery, sodomy, theft, murder, and all manner of mischiefs[.][95]

Considering these serious and far-reaching consequences of both male and female vowed virginity, it is unsurprising to find that the green-sickness, discussed in so many medical writings, also makes its way into literary portrayals of female virginity. Burton, for instance, claims that green-sickness affects virgins and nuns in particular, citing a range of authorities in his discussion of its symptoms.[96] The symptoms of green-sickness lent themselves to poetry, which could discuss them by referring to and playing with familiar literary conventions which were easily adapted to describe the condition of green-sick girls, usually in poems that praised their condition – but as a temporary one. The virgin who might be tempted to remain just that is warned that the lover will claim 'his right', for 'You were not born to serve your only will; / Nor can your beauty be perpetual'.[97] The threat of imminent decay is used to convince her that she must seize the moment (and lover) rather than risk outliving her shelf-life or acting selfishly.

The recommended path of action is sex. Virgins sicken once they reach adolescence; men are the cure. That, at least is the argument put forward in writings such as the 'Mournfull Ditty', which concludes the seventeenth-century *Virgins Complaint for the Loss of Their Sweethearts*. Allegedly '[p]rinted at the earnest request of many thousands of virgins' of England, the same virgins complain that the wars ravaging the country are depriving them of their rightful mates, wars 'far more ravenous and greedy than we *Maids* are after *Mans* flesh'. As a result, they are suffering terribly from green-sickness: '[T]he violence of our concupiscence driving us . . . into that consumption of the sweets of *Maiden-heads*, the green-sickness, which feed upon us more ravenously than a Vulture, deflowering and penetrating the precious colour of our complexions changed thereby into a bad and ill-favoured hue.' The ensuing 'hideous and deathful longings' drive them into the arms of unsuitable lovers in their frenzied desperation to be eased of 'this insupportable burden of our virginities'. They conclude with the ditty's bawdy plea:

> Tis not your glisters,
> Purges nor blisters
> Can make our sickly bodies whole and sound:
> No sleepy potion,
> Nor other notion
> Of Physick for our sickness can be found:
> Only one thing which makes us thus condole,
> The oil of man can cure us in the hole.[98]

Should they not receive the 'oil of man', their choices are twofold: they can either 'keep our maiden heads till they be musty', or they can become 'Martyrs in the flames of carnality and concupiscence'.[99]

In some representations, virginity is linked more overtly to death itself. In *A Midsummer Night's Dream*, for instance, Hermia is told that her disobedience to her father will result either in her death or in enforced lifelong virginity, which suggests that the two are comparable punishments. Theseus tells her that she must examine her 'youth' and ask herself whether:

> You can endure the livery of a nun,
> For aye to be in shady cloister mewed,
> To live a barren sister all your life,
> Chanting faint hymns to the cold, fruitless moon.

While he quickly adds that those who choose this life are to be commended for their 'maiden pilgrimage', this seems a rather half-hearted endorsement, particularly when he goes on to tell her that the rose who blooms on earth is happier than the one that 'wither[s] on the virgin thorn'.[100] In 'The Virgin Martyr' by Ada Cambridge (1844–1926), the association of death and virginity is made even more explicit: 'I, a young maid once, an old maid now, deposed, despised, forgotten . . . have thrilled with passion and have dreamed of nuptial rest, / Of the trembling life within me of my children unbegotten'.[101] Wifehood and motherhood are the natural conditions for a woman; those who stand outside clearly do so regretfully, seeing it as an enforced martyrdom. One of the most powerful literary descriptions that fuses the idealization of virginity and youth while also contrasting it to the monstrous uncanniness of aged virginity is found in Charles Dickens's *Great Expectations* (1861). When Miss Havisham, a reclusive and bitter old woman who has never recovered from her lover's desertion many years before, first summons the child Pip to her home, her grotesque appearance tells a story of frustrated youth and femininity. Entering her room with trepidation, Pip finds that his eyes need to adjust in the murky gloom; once they have, he is confronted with the 'strangest lady' he has ever encountered:

> I saw that everything within my view which ought to be white, had been white long ago, and had lost its lustre, and was faded and yellow. I saw that the bride within the bridal dress had withered like the dress, and like the flowers, and had no brightness left but the brightness of her sunken eyes. I saw that the dress had been put upon the rounded figure of a young woman, and that the figure upon which it now hung loose, had shrunk to skin and bone. Once, I had been taken to see some

ghastly waxwork at the Fair, representing I know not what impossible personage lying in state. Once, I had been taken to one of our old marsh churches to see a skeleton in the ashes of a rich dress, that had been dug out of a vault under the church pavement. Now, waxwork and skeleton seemed to have dark eyes that moved and looked at me. I should have cried out, if I could.[102]

Likened to a waxwork and a corpse, artifice and death meet to devastating effect in Miss Havisham. All the signs of virginity that make sense in relation to a young bride – pure yet sexual – such as the flowers, the white veil, the jewels, become grotesque when adopted by an aged woman. There are many versions of this in Western culture: the 'sterile virgin . . . the impotent old maid, the dried-up and ineffectual maiden aunt . . . the poisonous, vampire lesbian teacher or the monstrous female artist'.[103]

Endings

In that loss of virginity is perceived – for both men and women, though not in the same way – as a threshold moment, marking the transition into adulthood, it is intimately tied up with memory.[104] The remembering of the loss of one's virginity informs a whole literary and cinematic genre in itself, with its own conventions and familiar themes and plots, showing how such a supposedly individual and foundational experience is at least to some extent shaped through the narratives we are familiar with. In *The Virgin Suicides* (1993), a novel by Jeffrey Eugenides (filmed by Sofia Coppola in 2000), Mrs Lisbon, the strict, repressed Catholic mother of the five beautiful Lisbon girls tries ever more desperately to protect her daughters from a world that includes the sinful temptations of alcohol, cigarettes, pop music and, particularly, sex. When the most precocious of the girls, Lux, stays out long past her curfew after a school dance, Mrs Lisbon isolates the daughters completely by locking them up in the house. What she does not realize is that Lux has not only already lost her virginity but continues to have sex with a wide range of boys and men on the roof of the family home. A group of neighbourhood boys, of whom the narrator is one, becomes so obsessed with the girls that their memories of them continue to shape their lives long after the girls have killed themselves. As the grown-up narrator says, looking back on his adolescence: 'Years later, when we lost our own virginities, we resorted in panic to pantomiming Lux's gyrations on the roof so long ago'. Virginity is connected to memory in Western culture not least because it has been imagined for centuries as marking several crucial boundaries: between childhood and adulthood; innocence and experience; men and women; life and death. At the same time, as a symbol or as an identity it continues to resist easy or straightforward definition. When the narrator in *The Virgin Suicides* tries to describe how he and his friends spent years trying to make sense of the Lisbon girls, he resorts repeatedly to images of light. The 'glittering' girls come to represent every Western stereotype and fantasy of feminine mystery, from the 'phantasmagoria of beacons' shed by the votive candles the girls light in memory of their youngest sister, Cecilia, to the 'bordello glow' of sexy Lux's Chinese lantern.[105]

To the boys, the girls represent all that is desirable and mysterious about life. Their deaths only consolidate that obsession, preventing the young voyeurs from growing into a reality that can never match the blinding promises the past seemed to hold: 'The only way we could feel close to the girls was through these impossible excursions, which have scarred us forever, making us happier with dreams than wives.' In the end they are left with neither life nor memories: 'The truth was this: we were beginning to forget the Lisbon girls, and we could remember nothing else.' While the book is saturated with images of light – most evident in the naming of Lux – the light is not one that illuminates, but rather blinds or offers a blankness that equates with silence: 'And every other slide in our carousel began to fade in the same way, or we clicked and absolutely nothing fell into the projection slot, leaving us staring with goose bumps on a white wall.'[106] Overloaded with the meanings and with desires projected onto them by others – parents, teachers, men, neighbours, psychologists, doctors, boys, the narrator and readers – the girls metamorphose into semi-mythical creatures, capable of standing for everything and therefore also for nothing:

> More and more, people forgot about the individual reasons why the girls may have killed themselves, the stress disorders and insufficient neurotransmitters, and instead put the deaths down to the girls' foresight in predicting decadence. People saw their clairvoyance in the wiped-out elms, the harsh sunlight, the continuing decline of our auto industry.

The girls have to die; it is demanded by the logic of virginity. The 'pure' life their mother wants for them is really a living death; their deaths in turn freeze them in that ideal virginal state that fuels desire, fantasy and, as the book proves, art. *The Virgin Suicides* is a novel not just about virgins, or about suicides, or about rites of passage. It is about memories, about how meanings and stories begin, evolve and dissipate – all of them reflections and refractions, fragments rather than final and incontrovertible truths. It also narrates desire and loss, both of which are profoundly connected in Western culture with the pleasures of virginity and of narration: '[A]ll we could make out were the phosphorescent outlines of the girls' bodies, each a different glowing letter of an unknown alphabet.'[108]

4

'Repugnant to the Common Good'

*The same God that hath denied power to the hand to
speak, to the belly to hear, and to the feet to see, hath
denied to woman power to command man.*[1]

*No case can occur, in which public feeling is more
warmly or justly excited, than where an attempt is
made to injure or destroy the purity of the female.*[2]

Women who say no do not always mean no.[3]

The body politic

The virginal body is never just – or perhaps is simply never –
a *real* body; what we understand by it is always determined by
our cultural context and traditions. The ways in which virginity is thought about, however, affect the real lives of girls
and women. It is here, in the public sphere, that the political
becomes really personal. Virginity might not seem to have any
obvious connection to the world of politics or social governance, but how it was used by political thinkers as a concept,
and how it was enshrined in law, show how the abstract and the
concrete are, in fact, deeply indebted to one another, and how,

together, they influence the ways in which female sexuality is theorized and legislated.

In the medieval political poem 'The Descryvying of Mannes Membres', the writer explains how he imagines society – the body politic – as being comparable to the human body: 'I liken a kingdom in good condition, / To a man, vigorous in health'. He goes on to describe which part of the human body corresponds to which part of the body politic: for instance, the head is the king, who rules, and the feet are the peasants, who toil in the earth and support the rest of the body. (Even today we still refer to a political leader as 'the head of state'.)[4] This metaphor allows the writer to express a range of assumptions about the organization of society. Firstly, the human body needed all of its limbs to be healthy and function properly; secondly, all of the limbs had to work in harmony for the body to move as it was meant to. These stipulations memorably express the need for social health and social harmony. Should these criteria not be fulfilled, disease will follow, and there are always those waiting to exploit weakness:

> If each of his limbs argues with the others
> He grows sick, for flesh is frail.
> His enemies wait early and late,
> To creep up on him in his weakness.

The body as symbol for society also expresses other values central to medieval political theory: each 'member' has its divinely ordained place, which it must maintain for the body to stay healthy. What would happen if a foot (peasant) suddenly decided it was the head (king), and acted accordingly? No, a foot is and must stay a foot – like the human body, the order of the political body was understood to be divinely ordained and any attempt to change that order and hierarchy was unnatural and monstrous.

The writer does not stop at bodily health. He adds that God has created man in such a way that even if all his limbs are healthy, he still requires inner qualities in order for the whole to work:

> May God preserve this man who is thus designed
> Head and body, all limbs in accordance with nature.
> But those who despise virtues
> Waste their breath when they pray to God.[5]

Should the human/political body be sinful, disaster threatens and God will turn away, with dire consequences. Since the body in this theory also stands for the communal body, one can see that individual sin can never just be that: it will also affect the health of the body politic. This is why 'sins' such as heresy or rebellion (unless the king was a tyrant) were often described as diseases that threatened to destroy the body politic from the inside. This model of political theory was made familiar by John of Salisbury's twelfth-century advice book for princes, *Policraticus*, which has been called 'the first complete work of political theory written during the Middle Ages'.[6] The description of the body as a political paradigm also drew on medieval scientific ideas that saw the human body as a microcosmic version of the universal macrocosm, with each of the body's individual limbs and organs under the influence of a specific planet. In addition, each individual occupied a place in the social hierarchy, as well as having familial, communal and religious obligations. These ideas all reveal the intricate web of influences the human individual was caught up in: if he never acted out of complete independence because he, as microcosm, was caught up in wider structures, then his actions too could not be seen as purely individual, with no effect on those he was connected to in a range of relationships.

Political theorists made this point particularly with regard to the king who was, after all, the head that ruled the body. Several medieval writers emphasize the necessary virtue of the king, advising him to be chaste, as Thomas Hoccleve does in the fifteenth-century *Regement of Princes*. As an example of this, he tells the story of a young man whose beauty attracted much attention. Because he was virtuous, however, he wanted to deflect it and finally did so by lacerating his face with nails and with knives in order to avoid 'uncleanness'.[7] A politician's fitness to rule and his or her political integrity are still judged to some extent on personal conduct, not least in sexual matters. If the king's virtue – or lack of it – could have an impact on the health of his kingdom, then the 'health' of the body politic was, in turn, judged in relation to misdemeanours enacted by individual bodies. Some medieval legal writers, for instance, used the crime of rape to measure the spiritual health of the kingdom, whereby 'the safety of women in a kingdom is the mark of law and order, and of a good ruler'.[8] Others drew attention to the number of virgin martyrs a nation could boast of in order to show its exceptional qualities; for some kings, like England's Edward the Confessor (1042–66), virginity was part of their personal mystique (at least posthumously), linking the role of king with that of celibate saint.[9] Royalty in general repeatedly drew on the symbolism of virginity, especially in its self-representations in literature, its rituals and ceremonies.[10] A future queen had to be a virgin when she first married the king in order to guarantee the purity of the bloodline and the legitimacy of the heir; rumours that Lady Diana Spencer had a virginity test before she was deemed a suitable marriage candidate for Prince Charles echo this concern.

The best-known example of chaste rulership is not, however, that of a king, but of a queen. Elizabeth I famously used a virginal identity to make powerful and effective political claims. It enabled her to refuse suitors, thereby allowing her to

A sixteenth-century woodcut portrait of Queen Elizabeth I. The text beneath the image hails her as a 'pearl' – a familiar symbol of purity and virginity.

maintain the authority which she would have ceded to her husband had she married. In his 1586 account of Elizabeth's reign, the historian William Camden describes how a deputy from the Lower House came to her, voicing Parliament's anxiety about her unmarried status, for 'nothing can be more repugnant to the common good, than to see a Princess who by marriage may preserve the Commonwealth in peace, to lead a single life, like a Vestal Nun'. His Elizabeth, characterized by 'manly courage', responds with stern dignity:

> '[W]hen the public charge of governing the Kingdom came upon me, it seemed to me an inconsiderate folly, to draw upon myself the cares which might proceed of marriage. To conclude, I am already bound unto an Husband, which is the Kingdom of England . . .'
> (*And therwithall, stretching out her hand, she showed them the Ring with which she was given in marriage, and inaugurated to her Kingdom*[.])[11]

Like a more secular version of the 'Vestal Nun' feared by Parliament, she too was married – had given herself to – a higher entity than any mere individual man.[12] Virginity conveyed moral, spiritual and physical benefits that could be drawn on and wielded effectively, and it was to remain 'a powerful political weapon all through [Elizabeth's] reign'.[13] If the chaste king in Hoccleve embodies the qualities of good governance – control, sobriety and dominance of reason – then Elizabeth could add to these the feminine roles of wife (of England) and mother (of the English people).

Nonetheless, female rule was perceived as problematic, for virgins were still women and female virginity was associated with a range of other political discourses that did not sit comfortably with Early Modern ideas of strong rulership. In 1603, when James I acceded to the throne, to the relief of many who could not reconcile the two categories of 'woman' and 'ruler', he also drew on virginal symbolism; however, this time he was the virile man going to meet his virginal bride, England.[14] This was perceived by some thinkers of the seventeenth century to be a perfect symbol for the nation of the future. The idea of the 'virgin' state or nation being symbolized by a virgin – either as leader or as patron saint – is bound to encourage ideas of national purity, however that is then interpreted. We have seen how another famous virgin was used as a national symbol: Joan of Arc continues to be treated as representative of the French nation by a range of different and at times conflicting political groupings. She is, for instance, a favourite with Jean-Marie Le Pen, leader of the far-right French National Front, whose controversial ideas on immigration and Holocaust denial reveal the darker side of the pure, impermeable virgin's symbolic potential.[15]

Virgin territories

Describing territories or landscapes in terms of women's bodies and feminine qualities, particularly female fertility, was a familiar rhetorical move which occurs frequently in literary writings. It was also one used enthusiastically by those promoting colonization and conquest.[16] When Sir Walter Ralegh sought to persuade Elizabeth I that Guiana was a land ripe for the picking, he described it as a 'Country that hath yet her Maidenhead', having 'never been entered by any army of strength and never conquered and possessed by any Christian

Prince'. (He had at this point already talked about the 'Maidenhead of Peru'.)[17] The image of rapine is particularly piquant here in that the suggested ravisher of the Virgin Land would be a Virgin Queen. Similarly, the naming of the American colony of Virginia honours its 'virgin conqueror' while also implying that the land was 'unknown' before its colonization.[18] The fecund virgin land – like the nubile human virgin – needs to be possessed; without 'owner', she is free for the taking. Indeed, it is for her own good that she should be taken for, as we know, virgin soil needs to be 'tilled' to be fertile; the page needs to be inscribed in order to convey meaning. Colonization can thus be reimagined as an almost charitable act, performed for the good of the colony-to-be. This is evident in the following seventeenth-century comparison of Ireland to a girl suffering from green sickness:

> This Nymph of Ireland, is at all points like a young wench that hath the green sickness for want of occupying. She is very fair of visage, and hath a smooth skin of tender grass. It is now since she was drawn out of the womb of rebellion about sixteen years, by our Lady nineteen, and yet she wants a husband, she is not embraced . . .[19]

These images of conquest and despoliation, juxtaposed with those of seduction, in which the landscape becomes a desirable-but-helpless (or hapless) woman, are inverted in common terms for sexual intercourse or rape. In a study of terminology used by Early Modern French midwives, one critic describes how the raped female body is repeatedly compared by them 'to a territory attacked, an individual soldier conquered, mutilated, or in retreat, and a castle whose door was entered forcibly'. These analogies turn injured female genitalia into ransacked landscapes or buildings, with 'the neck of the womb cleaved, the lady of the middle (hymen) in retreat, the nymphs (labia minora) destroyed or sundered, the back ditch (cervix) opened, the neck of the womb split, the edge of labia peeled or flayed, the *os pubis* bone crashed, burst, broken to pieces, bruised, and crushed, and the clitoris flayed and skinned'.[20] Such associations are perhaps not surprising, considering that a brief look into a contemporary thesaurus will highlight the enduring connection between sex and violence. Synonyms for defloration, for instance, include 'assault, defile, desecrate, despoil, force, harm, mar, molest, rape, ravish, ruin, spoil, violate'.[21] When sexual and martial violence, two activities closely associated with masculinity, are linked both become normalized – they are part of what men do: boys will be boys. This makes it difficult to distinguish 'good' aggression from 'bad', for male violence can both protect and disrupt the social body.

The role that the individual body played in the welfare of the body politic was taken up and expanded on in Puritan thought. As one critic points out: 'post-Reformation civic rhetoric built upon an astringent moral discourse' in which the 'body politic and the godly citizen' were linked. This relationship between body politic and individual citizen was one of mutual influence: because the individual's probity affected that of the civic body, the latter had an interest – indeed, a right – to regulate the individual's behaviour. While men's threat to civic order was perceived to lie in the public sphere – in drunkenness or brawling – women's was far more likely to be located in relation to sins that were seen as private, especially sexual transgressions.[22] These sins were only private in the sense that they did not usually occur in public view; they were certainly considered to be of public interest, however, not least because improper sexual behaviour was thought to indicate a moral failing in the wider community.

One of the reasons why the male body was used as a model for the body politic in medieval and later political theory was that, in addition to being perceived as naturally destined for rulership, the male body was also understood as more 'closed' from outside influences than that of the woman, which leaked milk and blood and was open to penetration. Women's bodies therefore come to be seen 'as, literally, the entry by which the pure content may be adulterated'.[23] The 'pure content' that is polluted by penetration is not just the virgin's body itself. While the virginal body could figure as a closed body par excellence – it was repeatedly likened to an enclosed garden, a shut door, a sealed fountain, a fortified castle – being female nonetheless, it was also vulnerable to attack, both from within and without. Its seamless boundaries were coveted by those who sought to breach them, either by persuasion or by force. Innate female weakness made this even more likely. Thus the virgin was perceived as both particularly valuable and particularly vulnerable; as a man, you either wanted one as your bride, or, if she was your daughter, you made sure that others didn't get her without your permission. Virgins were contested social territory.

As the story of the Nun of Watton demonstrates (above, p. 37), the individual nun's loss of virginity and therefore purity was seen to compromise the purity of the whole community. Here, the boundaries of the young woman's body are mapped onto the boundaries of the religious community of which she is a member: the breaching of her body is also the breaching of that community. In the secular sphere, a woman's honour and the boundaries of her body were most immediately linked to the body of the family. With the heightened emphasis in Protestant thought on the importance of the family, a man's inability to keep his family 'in order' cast doubt on his own integrity and suitability for the public sphere. After all, as one writer puts it: 'An Household is as it were a little Commonwealth.' Since the family was understood as a microcosm of the kingdom, with the father at the head, the wife and children's behaviour (as his 'subjects') served as mirrors, reflecting either his competence or his impotence:

> [I]t is impossible for a man to understand how to govern the common-wealth, that doth not know to rule his own house, or to order his own person; so that he that knoweth not to govern, deserveth not to reign.

It is no good complaining about the state of society, if a man cannot regulate his own affairs: 'For such Householders as pretend to be great Protestants ... may long enough talk of Discipline, and still compain of the want of Church government; but all in vain, and to no purpose, unless they will begin this most necessary discipline, in reforming their own houses.'[24] Within this context, a daughter's transgression, particularly if it was sexual, brought with it serious repercussions. As Juan Vives warns in his immensely popular sixteenth-century *Instruction of a Cristen Woman*: 'Everyone shall think themselves dishonested by one shame of that maid: what mourners, what tears, what weeping of the father and mother and bringers up.' Not only does she bring shame upon her immediate family – her dishonour pollutes and disgusts all who know her:

What cursing will there be of her acquaintance, what talk of neighbours, friends, and companions, cursing that ungracious young woman; what mocking and babbling of those maidens that envied her before; what a loathing and abhorring of those that loved her; what fleeing of her company[.]

He predicts that all 'those that before sembled love' will now 'openly hate her' and 'cast the abominable deed in her teeth'. The maiden can hope for little after this: 'Let her that hath lost her virginity turn her which way she will, she shall find all things sorrowful and heavy'; he wonders 'how a young maiden seeing this can . . . have joy of her life at all'. Shame and the threat of ostracism, which are shown here to run like contagion through the community in relentless, ever-widening circles, are summoned to police the young woman's sexual behaviour; her body and desire are not hers to do with as she pleases, for her body possesses a significance and a worth that goes beyond the merely personal. Not only that, but Vives places the whole blame for this calamity on the woman, by opening his text with the observation that even hardened men of war and those inflamed by love and desire would not dream of deflowering a virgin: 'Every man is sore [afraid] to take away that which is of so great price.' (This begs the question how it is those shameless virgins actually lose their maidenheads.) It is clearly only a hardened woman who would care so little for what all others treasure. This uneven distribution of blame adds to the sense that not only is the virgin's body devalued, her whole family's public standing is threatened as well.

It is a small step from the public shame and symbolic emasculation that a daughter's – or wife's – sexual transgression is seen to perpetrate upon the men in her family, to violent retaliation and punishment by male members of the family in an effort to restore male honour. As Vives remarks: 'I know that many fathers have cut the throats of their daughters, brethren of their sisters, and kinsmen of their kinswomen.' He gives an example from Spain, where he knew of 'two brethren [who] thought their sister had been a maid' and, 'when they saw her great with child, they dissembled their anger as long as she was with child: but as soon as she was delivered of her child, they thrust swords into her belly and slew her, the midwife looking on.' In another example, the avengers of lost virginity are 'three maidens', who strangle their friend 'when they took her in the abominable deed'. Vives concludes that 'History is full of [such] examples and daily you see [them].'[25] This form of shame and the violence it unleashes is not, however, associated with male sexual behaviour; in a patriarchal system a profligate son is not punished in this way. Although excessive sensuality might be seen to compromise his manliness (for men should be guided by reason, not lust), and even if he is seen as a bit of an embarrassment (or, alternatively, as a 'chip off the old block'), his behaviour causes no real danger to family reputation, and there is therefore no need to restore family 'honour'.

Virginity in the marketplace

The 'fallen' girl's shame does not stem solely from spiritual considerations; there are important social, economic and political ramifications that hinge on female virginity and chastity.[26] Even as marriage and family became increasingly central to the ideology of the Early Modern state, this did not mean that virginity was passé; as has been pointed out in relation to Stuart England, 'virginity did not go out of style[;] rather, it was increasingly invoked as a social value regulating female sexuality'.[27] As early as the twelfth century, political power and authority became increasingly focused on the person of the king. With this came a greater emphasis on ancestry and bloodline: the legitimate heir to the throne would be, ideally, the king's eldest son. To whom one was related, and whom one married became critical – and political – issues.[28] Women's bodies were considered useful in cementing old alliances or shaping new ones, both internationally and locally. A virgin daughter did not only act as a mirror of her father's ability to control his family affairs; she could be a valuable asset in his economic and political dealings. In turn, because primogeniture structured the inheritance system – meaning that the eldest son inherited all – a prospective groom and his family wanted to ensure with absolute certainty that this heir would be legitimate. A virgin bride offered some guarantee. As we can see, the value of virginity was viewed very differently within the religious and the secular spheres. Where the church (ideally) viewed the virgin as 'a treasure saved up', the secular realm viewed her as a valuable commodity to be put into circulation. The former saw an offering to God; the latter a godsend for realpolitik.[29]

With the emergence of the bourgeois family, however, which some scholars locate in the late Middle Ages, primogeniture is not necessarily the way in which inheritance is ordered. This means that it is not just the virginity of the bride that is important; because the legitimacy of *all* children must be guaranteed, the ongoing chastity and fidelity of the wife also become central to family honour.[30] Vives concludes his chapter on the 'keeping of virginity and chastity' by reminding his female readers that he is aiming his advice not just at virgins, 'but also married women and widows and finally all women'. Wifely chastity is important, one eighteenth-century writer explains, because in her infidelity she

> imposes a spurious Breed on her Husband's Family; makes a Foreigner Heir to his Estate; depriving sometimes his own real Children begotten afterwards, of their just Inheritance; or, at least, his right Heirs and next Relations; but makes the Son of a Man his Heir, who has done him the greatest Injury.[31]

The problems of gaining detailed information about the poorest members of medieval society mean that the impact that loss of virginity had on such families is difficult to ascertain. Nonetheless, it appears that both the middle and lower-middle strata shared a firm investment in virginity; their daughters 'had attained the status of currency: items of exchange in which families had a strong interest, assessable for monetary value, to be saved up and spent in the marriage bed'.[32] However, in reality, many young women would never marry and lived as single women most, if not all, of their lives. Of these, those living in cities were usually poor – wages for women were very low – and vulnerable to accusations of unchastity, or having to be so due to the demands of their masters, or because of economic necessity. University students in the Middle Ages (who were all male), for instance, focused their sexual attentions on servants and prostitutes since they were warned not to get involved with married women or with women of equal status whom they might have to end up marrying.[33]

With changes in economic contexts, the role female chastity did – or could – play in a given class also shifted. In the eighteenth and nineteenth centuries, for instance, the proper sphere for women was thought to be the domestic one. Unlike the late medieval domestic situation, however, this did not involve the woman's active participation in the family business, which was increasingly separated from the home. The woman at home was to be idle, a sign of her husband's economic success, which in itself shows how this was an ideal that could not be a reality for everyone. Well-to-do homes ran on the work of servants, many of whom were poor women and therefore often vulnerable, particularly to sexual advances by their employers. The idealization of middle-class domesticity resulted in a double standard, not just between men and women, but also between women. As one critic points out, 'the ideological division of women into two classes, the virtuous and the fallen, was already well developed by the mid-eighteenth century'.[34] This insidious and complacent logic, which associates poor women with 'bad' sexual behaviour, and judges this to be primarily a moral failing, is still alive today.

Whereas in the Middle Ages and Early Modern period women were thought to be more sexually voracious than men, this changed in the eighteenth and nineteenth centuries, during which women became increasingly desexualized as they became domesticated. This 'domestic ideology', which was based on an idealization of the 'middle-class Protestant woman', lauded the woman's spiritual qualities: her more fully developed morality, her delicacy of feeling, her maternal responsibilities and her inner purity.[35] Thus, while men were 'the bearers of energy, vitality, and sexuality', women became 'the bearers of civilization'.[36] Female chastity was both pre-requisite and evidence of this lofty status. Although virginity was only important as a premarital state, *chastity* was to last forever. It was idealized as the very essence of womanhood, as one eighteenth-century writer explains to his female reader:

> Chastity is so essential and natural to your sex, that every dec-lination from it is a proportionable receding from womanhood. An immodest woman is a kind of monster, distorted from its proper form.[37]

The home environment was seen to safeguard and guarantee this chastity, both for the daughter and for the wife. Chaste maternity became the core identity that all women were to strive for, and so virginity was relegated to an ever more mar-ginal position: an important but transitional stage that could become a problem if it lasted too long. Thus, although the ear-lier view of the sexual woman gave way to some extent, it did not disappear entirely. It was used to stigmatize women who did not conform to the domestic ideal, either because of class, religion, nationality, or because of a desire for a life that lay outside such strict parameters.[38] Two such types of woman for nineteenth-century Protestant America were the nun and the prostitute, who became conflated in their perceived deviance from the norm. It is not surprising, therefore, that anti-Catholic propaganda – whether in Early Modern England or in nineteenth-century America – focused on portraying monasteries and convents as houses of sin and iniquity.[39] Perhaps the most notorious example of these 'convent narratives' – a reaction in part to the influx of a large number of Catholic immigrants – is a book called *The Awful Disclosures of Maria Monk* (1836), purportedly an autobiography about the author's time in the Hôtel Dieu convent in Montreal. Its disclosures titillate the reader with lurid stories of the repeated rape of nuns by lascivious priests, the murders of the innocent infants that are the result of these illicit copulations, and the sadistic humiliations of a sexual nature instigated mainly by the Mother Superior, including whippings, the infamous 'hot plug' treatment (in which a large wooden phallus covered in an astringent paste is inserted anally), and even the execution of those nuns who resist such treatment. The book was a raging success, even though its contents were discredited not long after its publication.[40]

If the middle-class mother bore and raised children imbued with the values considered desirable, one can see that the nun and the prostitute could both be perceived as weakening the body politic: the former in her rejection of the roles of wife and mother; the latter as home destroyer and carrier of disease (both moral and physical). In the nineteenth century, this anxiety also extended to working-class women, especially those who worked in the factories; one critic notes that 'this is reflected in the way reformers, for example, portrayed factory work as fraught with perils of seduction and violation and where the bourgeois discourse of seduction regarded both a seduced woman and a rape victim as fundamentally fallen.'[41] Chastity and 'virginal modesty', in turn, were explained as inherent in the woman, as natural to women, and thus independent from any external circumstances such as culture or religion:

That this Modesty is from their [women's] Nature, if not perverted, is evident from all Accounts of the ancient Heathens,
and the most barbarous Nations, where a virginal Modesty still
appears in them, abstracting from Religion, and external
Education[.][42]

By presenting it as a timeless and universally recognized truth,
the writer silences any opposing view: virginal modesty is simply
there, an undisputed fact; if it wasn't there, its absence signalled
a serious flaw in nature. This meant that all those women who
were considered 'immodest' could also be labelled – and treated
as – 'perverted' and 'unnatural'. At the same time virginity – at
least maintained virginity – could also be seen as a rejection of
'natural' womanhood and its duties towards family and society.

The public woman

In the nineteenth and early twentieth centuries women who
rejected or challenged a purely domestic role were perceived as
stepping outside the proper bounds designated for the female
sex. Those engaged in fighting for women's rights in particular
were viewed as a threat – not just to the social order, but
to the very health and 'womanliness' of the women themselves.
Women's efforts to gain greater access to the public sphere were
criticized and opposed by an impressive array of expert opinion,
not least from the medical establishment. Rather than just focusing on the threat women were thought to pose to the order of
the body politic, the increasingly influential medical profession
was used to persuade and warn women that they were damag-
ing themselves as well as their families and the nation. As Haller
and Haller show, '[m]edical men warned . . . that feminism

had destroyed much of woman's inherited immunity through efforts to imitate the male. General paralyses from overwork or prolonged worry, neurasthenia, insanity, crime, and alcoholism were making fearful inroads into the gentle sex.'[43]

Education and work were both threats to women's health and, by extension, to the survival of the (white) race and civilization. Because women had been increasingly associated

This image from a book called *Our Baby's History* (1903) is an illustrative example of how motherhood and female domesticity were increasingly idealized and sentimentalized.

with the task of civilizing the aggressive and active male, as well as being responsible for instilling the correct moral and civic values in their children, any attempt to be active beyond the domestic sphere was bound to result in social degeneration or even disintegration.[44] What about the woman who did not want to marry, or who did pursue an education, or who did not believe that maternity was her sole destiny?[45] One authority viewed menstruation as 'nature's warning to the mannish maiden that any effort to avoid her biological responsibilities was a crime against womanhood and the community'. Education was therefore potentially problematic. While *some* education was a good thing – at least for those in the middle and upper classes – *too much* education could have disastrous consequences. One of these was that women who had been educated for too long would lose their interest in being wives and mothers, but not because it had opened up new horizons for them; medical opinion ventured that prolonged education led to a range of emotional and physical defects. As one guide, *Sex in Education; or, a Fair Chance for Girls*, points out, with reference to medical evidence, women who ignore nature's demands 'are [all] punished by similar weaknesses, degeneration, disease'. In addition, a highly educated woman would take on masculine character traits which would frighten men off; as a result of this, these men would end up visiting prostitutes and marrying women from lower social classes, which would result in an overall weakening of the race.[46] Others argued that heightened intellect in mothers would diminish their fertility, or result in less intelligent offspring.[47]

Some critics of the women's movement (which was very diverse) believed that the call for equal rights would result in a reversal of evolution, causing Western civilization to slip back into barbarism and savagery. Those women who wanted to move beyond the domestic sphere would, some predicted gloomily, become either 'mehitabels with voracious sexual appetites or depersonalized neuters'.[48] Similar views are already articulated in some medieval medical writings, where it was argued that the naturally weaker and imperfect physiology of the woman meant that any 'male' pursuits would endanger her health.[49] Late-medieval conduct books also warned women that if they wanted to ensure that their reputation stayed intact, they should avoid being seen out and about.[50] One can see why Joan of Arc caused such a scandal, breaking with authoritative opinion (as well as law) on gender, social and religious hierarchies. Her exceptional behaviour was put down either to sanctity or witchcraft. This uncertainty about her status extended to an uncertainty about her body – if she acted the way she did, could she really be a woman? The writer of one fifteenth-century text tells us that Joan's naked body was shown 'to all the people' before she was immolated, in order 'to take away any doubts from people's minds'. These doubts were to be mitigated by displaying 'the secrets that could or should belong to a woman'.[51] In stepping outside the roles through which femininity was defined in medieval culture, Joan became a troubling puzzle.

The emphasis on domesticity and associated traits of modesty, silence and obedience meant that any *public* appearance of a woman could cast doubt on her virtue. Terms such as 'public woman' or 'woman of the town' reveal how visibility and sexual availability are connected. In the Middle Ages women, while perhaps actively engaged in familial economies as well as exercising power over households (especially in the absence of husbands or other men), were not allowed to hold a public position. This prohibition was based on both secular and religious grounds: 'Secular law justified this on the grounds that women were by nature light-minded, wily, avaricious and of limited intelligence. Ecclesiastical law justified it on the grounds of Original Sin.'[52] And when women made a claim for their right to engage in the public sphere, most notably in the fight for women's suffrage in the nineteenth and twentieth centuries, there were those who denounced them as loose, or as masculinized viragos. It was not until 1918 that women won the right to vote in Britain; in the US it was 1920. Those who opposed women's activity in the public realm in later centuries gave similar reasons to those opposed to it in the Middle Ages. In addition, it was emphasized that women *were* valued and respected members of society, but that their duty lay in the home and that this was their natural sphere of influence. Those who strayed beyond the wholesome security of the domestic environment risked speculation over their mores, regardless of how 'respectable' they were.[53] As Sir James Elphinstone, MP, said about the politically active women questioning the sexual double standard as encapsulated in the Contagious Diseases Act in nineteenth-century Britain: 'I look upon these women who have taken up this matter as worse than the prostitutes'.[54]

Concerns that connect women's visible presence and engagement in the public sphere with male anger and violence have not disappeared. In fact, there is today a particular genre – related to that of self-help – which voices very clearly the concern that feminism has 'taken things too far', and that virginity is the solution to this problem. Wendy Shalit in *A Return to Modesty* argues that it is the loss of the virtue of

An image from a 1912 pro-suffrage work, entitled *Votes and Wages*, highlights the disempowerment of female workers.

female modesty as a result of feminism and sex education that has resulted in the increase of male disrespect for and violence against women: 'Female modesty gave men a frame of reference for a woman's "no"'. Shalit uses examples from literature to argue that, in the past, women were free from sexual harassment. In this unspecified and idealized past 'modesty . . . made every woman a lady, [and] male honor was what made every male a man'. Women should return to modesty, for this is the only way they can hope to change male behaviour: 'Woman can't tell men how to behave – they either inspire or fail to inspire.'[55]

Wendy Keller takes a different but related approach in *The Cult of the Born-Again Virgin*. She argues that 'we're realizing at last that the sexual freedom we have given ourselves since the 1960s might not be working for us anymore. It isn't getting us what we thought it would. We've thirty years of it – a long enough test.'[56] There are interesting assumptions here: first of all, that 'sexual freedom' suddenly happened (for everyone!) in the 1960s – as if traditional attitudes to sex could really be cast aside overnight – and then that thirty years can provide any reliable scale against which to measure change. Like Shalit, Keller argues that abstinence makes women stronger, allowing them the space to define what it is they want from a partner – but also from life more generally. In this, the two books are part of a tradition that sees virginity or abstinence as empowering for women, precisely because it allows them to escape or defer the demands of heterosexual sex and marriage.[57] This aspect is more strongly evident in Keller's book, which is not arguing for a return to a mythical past, and is not focusing primarily on waiting for the right man. Yet both can be read as reflecting a wider (and certainly not new or even particularly recent) cultural anxiety about gender roles, especially in times that are perceived as threatening or mercenary and soulless. One of the more curious things that Keller says is this: 'I call these women born-again virgins – women who have *returned* to the state of purity and control over their own bodies most of us knew as *girls*' (my emphasis). This call for a return to an idealized childhood purity, made by an adult woman in the name of female empowerment, seems to me odd and troubling. Keller, like Shalit, associates the fruits of feminism with male violence:

> While some will dispute Shalit's assessment that we have 'wiped clean all traces' [of patriarchal rule], we cannot deny that the fear factor for most women has increased dramatically. We now accept we must be afraid of rape, stalking, harassment, and in every other way used, manipulated, discarded, and unloved. We literally have created our own beds and now we lie in them. If this is equality and liberty, then perhaps we should find the middle ground, collectively and individually.[58]

Both Shalit and Keller to some extent lay the blame for what they perceive as a surge in male violence against women at the door of women – and both relate it explicitly to female sexual conduct.[59] It is therefore worth looking more closely at Shalit's argument that virginal modesty protects women from male sexual violence, and at how – in the context of the relationship between private and public bodies – individual female virginity (or 'modesty') figures in the law.

The virgin and the law: rape

One of the ways in which a society expresses and enforces its norms is through its laws. The law is there to protect both the individual and the public body, but at times it cannot avoid reflecting the prejudices and preconceptions of its writers and enforcers. In legal texts, virginity is discussed mainly in relation to rape, a crime whose definition has shifted, first from bodily injury to damage of property and then eventually to our modern idea of it as sexual violation without consent. What is evident in the legal treatises that deal with rape, and by extension also with questions of female sexual conduct, is that they draw heavily on medical, religious and literary representations of virginity and chastity in order to formulate their own definitions.

The crime of rape is of course neither acted out nor understood by any of those affected by it (whether victim, perpetrator, judge, jury or wider society) in a vacuum. It is interpreted in relation to a wide range of other ideas and assumptions prevalent in a given culture at a given time – beliefs, for example, about 'will and consent, morality, virtue, purity, ownership, authority, property, evil and forgiveness'. While these ideas change both through time and exist in a range of forms at any given moment, there are similarities that resonate across centuries. As one critic has remarked, 'many modern rape myths find their origins in the medieval period'.[60]

Medieval definitions of rape varied, depending on whether the sources one looks at are secular, religious or popular; nonetheless there is common ground. The root of the word 'rape', from the Latin *raptus*, translates as 'theft' or 'seizure', and was 'used in Roman law to denote abduction'.[61] In medieval England there were three legal traditions concerning rape that came together, more or less smoothly. After the Norman Conquest of 1066, English rape law changed gradually. Anglo-Saxon law had defined rape primarily as a crime of 'sexual violation' which could affect both virgins and non-virgins.[62] By the twelfth century, however, it was understood (in closer alignment with continental definitions) as '"ravishment", which might comprise either rape or abduction or both'.[63] The distinction between rape as physical violation and abduction became increasingly blurred in the later Middle Ages. The growing emphasis on abduction, which might or might not also involve sexual violation, reflects the pre-eminence of the view of *raptus* as a property crime, whose main victim was not the woman herself but rather her father, husband or other male relatives.[64] Whereas rape had previously counted as a felony (punishable by death or emasculation and blinding), and abduction merely as trespass, by 1487 this had changed; now abduction was the more serious offence, 'with or without defloration'.[65]

How rape was defined now also depended on *who* was

A fourteenth-century illumination showing a man trying forcefully to abduct a resisting woman. It accompanies a text on ecclesiastical law.

being violated: the rape of virgins was viewed by some (the Church, for instance) as a particularly heinous crime. It is worth quoting 'Bracton', the influential thirteenth-century legal authority, at length:

> Among other appeals there is an appeal called the rape of virgins. The rape of virgins is a crime imputed by a woman to the man by whom she says she has been forcibly ravished against the king's peace. If he is convicted of this crime [this] punishment follows: the loss of members, that there be member for member, for when a virgin is defiled she loses her member and therefore let her defiler be punished in the parts in which he offended. Let him lose his eyes which gave him sight of the maiden's beauty for which he coveted her. And let him lose as well the testicles which excited his hot lust. Punishment of this kind does not follow in the case of every woman, though she is forcibly ravished, but some other severe punishment does follow, according as she is married or a widow living a respectable life, a nun or a matron, a recognized concubine or a prostitute plying her trade without discrimination of person, all of whom the king must protect for the preservation of his peace, though a like punishment will not be imposed for each.[66]

It follows that if some women were granted special status as victims of rape others, such as prostitutes, were excluded or marginalized. In the case of defloration, some commentators recommended marriage between the rapist and the victim – with the agreement of all parties – as a satisfactory resolution to the situation. What is evident in these definitions is the conception of women as property, to be ranked in a specific hierarchy indicative of the level of damage that has been done to their respective value. *Raptus* is not an absolute – its quality and therefore its punishment depend less on the act itself than on who the victim is. Saunders summarizes it thus: '[T]he abduction, with or without her consent, of a virgin, widow or nun represents the gravest crime of *raptus*; the defloration of virgins or widows outside the context of abduction and irrespective of consent is ranked next as *stuprum*; the rape of wives is placed lowest on the scale as fornication, since, in this case, sex, even if non-consensual, does not decrease the woman's value.'[67] The question of consent, at the heart of modern Western definitions of rape, is largely irrelevant here.

'Consent' is a fraught term, and while its role was not as central to medieval definitions of rape as it is to ours today, its problematic nature was nevertheless thought to merit debate.[68] Theologians, concerned with theorizing vice and virtue, were particularly interested in discussing the question of will: it was here that the role of consent was explored most avidly, often in relation to the scenario of the raped virgin. What excited the intellect of these writers was whether the raped virgin could still claim to be a virgin if she did not consent to her violation in spirit. Although there was a strong tradition of religious authorities – going back to St Augustine – who said that in this case the virgin was indeed still a virgin (even a martyr), others were more doubtful, arguing that a woman could not ever be fully trusted to have resisted to the end, considering that she was by nature sensual and lascivious. Because of her perceived 'instinct for pleasure', these writers believed that even if the virgin might have resisted in spirit initially, it was likely that enjoyment would ultimately overwhelm her, thus rendering the violation agreeable to her. As a result, the woman had to be able to prove her wholehearted unwillingness – a difficult thing to do, as movements of the spirit are not easily made visible to doubters. Thus the '[r]ape of a virgin came to be viewed not as a crime for which the perpetrator was to be punished, so much as a circumstance whereby a woman's spiritual strength and purity were tested'.[69] This view is a persistent one. In the nineteenth century, we find Thomas Cooper stating his doubt that 'full' rape could ever occur without a woman's consent:

> [T]he consummation of a rape, by which is meant a complete, full, and entire coition, which is made without any consent or mission of the woman, seems to be impossible, unless some very extraordinary circumstances occur: for a woman always possesses sufficient power, by drawing back her limbs, and by the force of her hands, to prevent the insertion of the penis into her body, *whilst she can keep her resolution entire*.[70]

His final words reveal his doubt that a woman can indeed be resolute in her resistance to sexual violation. Or, in Judge Wild's words to the jury in a 1982 rape trial:

> Women who say no do not always mean no . . . If she doesn't want it she only has to keep her legs shut and she would not get it without force and then there would be the marks of force being used.

Helena Kennedy concludes that such views reveal a profound and deeply ingrained 'failure of understanding' of rape.[71]

In practice, it appears that even in periods in which rape was regarded as a felony, and in which the secular law at least recommended a capital punishment, those accused of rape were rarely punished according to the letter of the law, not least because conviction rates were very low. In contrast, compensation in the form of payment of fines to the victim's family occurred more frequently, often outside the context of the courts.[72] This, in turn, meant that success in receiving compensation – as well as the determination of the amount – depended on the power of the family involved, not boding well for the poor or women without family protection and support. While the return to a distinction between rape and abduction in sixteenth-century law might have suggested that the law once more prioritized the violation of the person over that of property, the reality remained bleak: 'Convictions for rape continued to be very rare and almost always involved the rape of a child or a young girl whose virginity was presumed forfeited.'[73] Furthermore, even though virgins were (at least on paper) no longer the only women to be considered victims of rape, the question of the victim's reputation remained central; behaviour that could be interpreted as flirtatious was then blamed for enflaming men's natural desires, or for sending out mixed signals. Because men's sexual behaviour was widely assumed to be active by nature, rape could then be interpreted as 'an extreme expression' of that.[74] In contrast, women's sexuality was most usually described in a language that associated it with sinfulness and, by extension, with whoredom: that is, *any* sexual act that a woman engaged in was potentially suspect. This meant, once more, that the onus was on the woman to prove her innocence, while the man's behaviour was rationalized in many instances as misguided – but understandable – virility.

An additional problem was that until the eighteenth century, Galenic ideas about procreation (see Chapter 1) informed legal writers. As Galen stated that a woman could only fall pregnant if she had achieved orgasm, this meant that any raped woman who fell pregnant after her violation – even a woman who was generally accepted to have been impecca bly virginal and innocent prior to the rape – had no defence as the pregnancy provided physical evidence that she had enjoyed the violation. In his immensely influential *Historia Placitorum Coronæ (History of the Pleas of the Crown)*, published in 1736, Sir Matthew Hale writes: 'And therefore that opinion of Mr. Finch, cited by *Dalton ubi supra*, and by *Stamford, cap.* 14, *fol.* 24, out of *Britton*, that it can be no rape, if the woman conceive with child, seems to be no law.'[75] Yet as late as 1819, Sir William Oldnall Russell, citing Hale, still finds it necessary to point out that 'the notion that if the woman conceived it could not be a rape, because she must, in such a case, have consented, appears to be quite exploded'.[76]

Proof of purity – or of absence of consent – meant that a woman had to be able to give visible evidence of her resistance, even if (or precisely because) resistance could heighten the level of violence used against her. This kind of evidence was primarily understood as physical evidence, visible on the body of the woman, in the form of injuries. As we have seen, however, physical loss of virginity cannot be ascertained with any finality. In 1823, Theodric Romeyn Beck writes in his discussion 'Of the signs of defloration and rape' that it is harder to detect physical evidence of rape in both 'married women [and] libidinous females'. It is unclear whether the latter category excludes virgins by definition, or suggests that there might be women, virgins or not, whose sensual natures mean that their bodies are not injured by violation. Is libidinousness a physical or a moral category here? As to *why* this difficulty of detection should exist, he remains opaque, despite having acknowledged the ambiguities in detecting, for instance, clear physical evidence for lost virginity. He merely states coyly: 'The reasons for this will readily suggest themselves.'[77] One assumes he means the size and condition of the vagina.

Yet this also proves problematic. In his work *Legal Medicine* (1882) Charles Meymott Tidy is of the opinion that

> Size of vagina is not to be relied upon for, as Duchatelet points out, the vagina may be as large in girls who have only recently become prostitutes, as in married women who have had a family; whilst on the other hand, the vagina in some prostitutes of twelve or fifteen years' standing has been observed to be as small as the vagina in virgins.[78]

Differences between the three wearyingly familiar categories of virgin/wife/whore are shown to be difficult – if not impossible – to ascertain on the physical evidence of their genitalia, yet the condition of the vagina is precisely what is meant to reveal the truth of their allegation of rape. Thus, while a woman's identity is defined according to the condition of her vagina – virgin (never penetrated), wife (penetrated by husband), prostitute (penetrated by many) – the difference between them, which is perceived to be of crucial importance in the social realm, is impossible to ascertain, closing the vicious circle of this impossible logic. Tidy continues his comparison between the virgin and the prostitute; while these two identities are supposed to exist at the furthest opposite extremes of the spectrum of female identities they are shown to be indistinguishable from one another:

Nor can *general appearance of genitals* be relied upon, for the same authority has recorded how in a female, æt. 51, who since 15 had been a woman of the town, the genital organs presented an *almost virginal appearance.*[79]

Not only that: those signs of virginity thought to be 'as a rule undoubtedly characteristic of virgins' are also not to be relied upon as they 'might be destroyed by self-abuse'. Does 'self-abuse', when it results in loss of the visible signs of virginity, mean that the virgin is 'libidinous'? And, if so, does that mean that it is difficult to detect signs of rape on her? Does this take us back to the idea that *all* women are, at heart, libidinous? And is a 'self-abusing' virgin still 'modest'? And where is one to look for 'proof', if the body is not to be trusted?

Still, the students of law need not worry unduly, for virgins are unlikely to be raped or, if they are, it will be evident. This, at least, is what seems to be suggested by Marshall Davis Ewell's definitions of defloration and rape respectively, in *A Manual of Medical Jurisprudence* (1887):

By 'defloration' is meant the act of depriving a female of her virginity; and by 'rape' is meant carnal knowledge of a woman by force and against her will. Cases of the former will seldom come before the medical jurist.[80]

Even those who concede that rape should be considered a crime whether the victim is a virgin or a prostitute maintain that her trustworthiness as a victim (and as a witness in court) depends on her sexual history. Andrew Ellison argues at the end of the nineteenth century that a woman who claims to have been a virgin prior to the rape should be questioned on this in order to ascertain her credibility as a witness:

> If she claims she was a virgin when raped, and especially if some of the evidence offered by the state tends to prove it, in my judgment the defendant should be permitted to prove specific acts of lewdness of the woman, not to justify the rape, if one was committed, but to place the entire case before the jury so that they may be better judges of the credibility of the witness.[81]

It should also be borne in mind that she might well have ulterior motives in claiming she was raped. In line with the medieval belief that women's speech was often false, fickle and cunning, Sir Matthew Hale, writing in the seventeenth century, says this of the rape victim as witness:

> It is true rape is a most detestable crime, and therefore ought severely and impartially to be punished with death; but it must be remembered, that it is an accusation easily to be made and hard to be proved, and harder to be defended by the party accused, tho never so innocent.[82]

These words are followed by Hale's recounting of numerous horror stories of scheming vixens who falsely accused innocent men.

Hale's warning was effective. Referring to it, Amos Dean reminds us in the mid-nineteenth century that 'As the person injured is the witness and sometimes the only one, a great many assignable motives may operate upon her mind to make that out a crime in another which will exonerate her from all personal blame.'[83] And in the early twentieth century we find W. G. Aitchison Robertson still echoing Hale faithfully: 'The commission of rape is often set up to hide the downfall of a young girl who wishes to avoid her disgrace. Again false charges of rape are sometimes made by women who are already pregnant.'[84]

What would it take for a woman to be able to convince a jury of her innocence? Hale outlines the following necessary conditions:

> [I]f the witness be of good fame [reputation], if [when] she presently discovered the offense made pursuit after the offender, showed circumstances and signs of the injury . . . if the place, wherein the fact was done, was remote from people, inhabitants or passengers, if the offender fled for it; these and the like are concurring evidences to give greater probability to her testimony, when proved by others as well as herself.

However,

> [I]f she concealed the injury for any considerable time after she had opportunity to complain, if the place, where the fact was supposed to be committed, were near to inhabitants, or common recourse or passage of passengers, and she made no outcry when the fact was supposed to be done, when and where it is probable she might be heard by others; these and the like circumstances carry a strong presumption, that her testimony is false or feigned.[85]

In other words, the 'true' rape victim must: (a) either be

virginal or chaste; (b) be clear-headed enough to pursue or cause others to pursue her offender shortly after her violation; (c) ensure she is raped in a remote place; (d) ensure that her attacker flees the scene of the crime; (e) make sure that, despite the remoteness of the location, there are others who can testify to her good character and her version of the events. Since her body – like her version of events – cannot be relied upon, the conditions for a favourable verdict for the victim become ever more remote, even if she is a virgin or a 'good girl'.

It is therefore not surprising that many women are afraid to report having been raped, or state that the trial is in some ways as traumatic as the original experience. Sue Lees, writing about England in the late 1990s, observes that 'rape trials today can be seen as both operating a warning, and a way of restricting the activities of women through inciting fear of the public sphere, but also through punishing a victim for breaking the silence enforced by the emphasis on female respectability and chastity'. In her study she shows how girls are still policed through reputation. She found that English adolescents in the 1990s distinguished between two types of girls, based on the 'difference between slags (whores, promiscuous girls) and drags (marriageable respectable girls)'. This is a lose-lose situation. As one of the girls she interviews says: 'It's a vicious circle. If you don't like them they'll call you a tight bitch. If you go with them then they'll call you a slag afterwards.'[86] Even not 'going with them' can lead to rumours that cast the girl concerned as a 'slag': all that needs to happen is that a boy tells his friends he *has* had sex with her. What the girl does – or does not do – often has little to do with the label she is given. And even if the girl *did* have sex, the fact that she can be stigmatized so effectively reveals the devastating power of such stubborn stereotypes.

It was not until the 1970s that women gained greater legal protection, not least because the women's movement began to criticize traditional rape law in the 1960s, highlighting its bias in favour of protecting the man accused rather than the victim. In the US this included the so-called 'rape shield laws', which seek to restrict the ways in which the complainant can be questioned about her past sexual conduct and her past relationship with the accused.[87] Such questions often sought to insinuate that the woman must have consented to sex with the accused, or pointed out that she was not trustworthy due to her sexual history.[88] While English law was changed in 2000 to disallow questioning of a woman's sexual past, as it was shown that this often led to a discrediting of the victim, barrister Vera Baird, QC, stated in 2005 that many judges had found ways of circumventing that, which means that it remains an issue of concern.[89] A 2005 Home Office study entitled 'A Gap or a Chasm? Attrition in Reported Rape Cases' showed that rape convictions in England and Wales had reached 'an all-time low': in 2003 the figure of those convicted was merely 5 per cent.[90] In 2005 the BBC reported, also with reference to this study, that reasons for such appalling figures lay in the attitude of many prosecutors and police, who 'did not believe victims' and subscribed to many rape myths.[91] Her experience in the English courts of the twentieth century led Helena Kennedy to conclude the following at that century's close:

Judges to this day advise juries in the language of our old misogynist friend, Sir Matthew Hale, that the accusation of rape is one that is easily made and, once made, difficult to defend, even if the accused is innocent. In my experience the reverse is true: the charge is hard to bring, but easy to defend.[92]

It remains to be seen whether the twenty-first century will offer anything different.

5

The Future of Virginity

Sexual politics

Sex and politics have a long and intimately entwined history; they share in turn a close proximity with scandal. The most famous recent example of this unholy trinity must be the Clinton-Lewinski scandal. One would have thought that politicians would learn to be more careful about preaching 'values' to the public, as it seems to result inevitably in public exposure of their own personal misdemeanours. John Major's Tory government had hardly uttered the words 'Back to Basics' before the media revealed that the 'basics' many of them were getting back to were rather different from those they were urging upon the public. In more recent times we see the Republicans in the US caught in a scandal in which a congressman campaigning to protect children from sexual predators was exposed as having sent explicit emails to adolescent boys. The nexus of sex and politics is fraught not least because it continually crosses the boundaries of 'private' and 'public'.

The idea of modern individual identity – and what it means to *be* an individual – has become absolutely inextricable from sexual identity. At the same time, not all identities are equal. Certainly those who do not conform to accepted – or dominant – modes of behaviour are vulnerable to discrimination and even persecution. While, on the one hand, individual choice is at the core of capitalist ideology, on the other, community or national welfare must also be considered in the governance of a body politic. Yet how this is done is a complex and often fraught issue, as it cannot avoid engaging in – and being shaped by – a wide spectrum of different and, at times, opposed agendas, for instance with prevailing beliefs about morality, religion, education, cultural, national welfare, gender, sexuality and racial issues. The nineteenth century in particular witnessed a multitude of turbulent discussions around sexuality, the law and the body politic. Certainly accelerated social change, economic instability and political insecurity precipitate widespread concern with sexual behaviour – usually with sexual morality or, rather, immorality.

In the nineteenth century, rapid industrialization, urbanization, the growth of urban poverty, economic depression and the changing role of women all contributed to concerns with 'social purity' and public morality. Jeffrey Weeks reminds us that 'then, as today, the family, demarcated sex roles and religion were promiscuously evoked as a necessary antidote to sexual chaos'.[1] Certainly, individual sexual acts were not seen as private in the sense of separable from the 'common good'. Fear over venereal disease, over proliferation of the 'wrong' kinds of people (mainly the poor),[2] declining birth rates – these and other anxieties fed in and came out of debates along with the new ideas emerging due to, for instance, Darwinism, sexology, social purity movements, women's rights and eugenics. Some of the most heated and formative debates at the time resulted in odd alliances, in complex and at times contradictory agendas, preventing any simple separation of interest groups along clear political lines.[3] Arguably, none of those movements was specifically interested in virginity, even if there was a very real concern about chastity.

The term 'social purity' indicates a concern for the 'purity' of both the individual and the social body. One area in which questions of politics, sexuality, morality, legislation and education continue to intersect in emotive and explosive ways is undoubtedly over the question of sex education of adolescents. The commonly voiced idea by conservative commentators that there was an absolute (and catastrophic) break with 'traditional' values concerning sexual behaviour in the 1960s and 1970s is fallacious: virginity, for instance, continued to be an important marker of personal and social identity throughout the decades following the 1960s. Even if there was a gradual movement towards viewing it as an embarrassment for girls as well as boys in the 1980s and 1990s, it was still acknowledged as an identity and the loss of it as a rite of passage. One critic suggests that because loss of virginity is 'widely perceived as one of the most significant turning points in sexual life' (which in turn means that it becomes an important issue for 'public health and policy professionals'), it functions as a focal point for anxieties prevalent in society, as well as a point of contention between groups with different approaches or agendas.[4]

While some commentators still claim that in the West, 'a

young woman's virginity is [merely] fodder for moral debate, parental worry, and giggly columns in teen magazines',[5] so-called virginity movements are becoming increasingly politically powerful and successful in such countries as the United States, where the Bush administration has ploughed millions of dollars into abstinence-only sex education in schools. The message to adolescents is that maintaining your virginity protects you not just from early pregnancy, but is the *only* reliable means of avoiding a bewildering and frightening plethora of sexually transmitted diseases. In addition, its proponents claim that virgins are mentally healthier: more independent, with higher self-esteem and therefore more likely to succeed socially and economically. Today in the US, virginity is at the heart of a battle being waged over sex education. Its consequences, however, will be felt internationally.

Teaching innocence

The sex education agenda that has been hailed by its supporters as a triumph for 'values', while being slated by its opponents for being antediluvian, is called 'abstinence education', or 'abstinence-only education'. It is the agenda that has once more turned 'virginity into a matter of public health, not just private morality'.[6] While there are different varieties of abstinence education, the central message is seemingly straightforward:

> [A]bstinence is refraining from sexual intercourse: those who have never had sexual intercourse should not initiate sexual intercourse; those who have had sexual intercourse should refrain from having further sexual intercourse.[7]

This is the message at the heart of abstinence education, even though the curricula associated with it have been refined over the past years. It is seen by its supporters as a radical response to a range of social problems, mainly centring on the behaviour of adolescents. What concerns policy-makers, educators, parents and religious groups alike are statistics such as the following:

> Teenage birth rates in the Unites States are higher than those of other Western industrialized nations, and out-of-wedlock births account for 7 out of 10 births to American women under age 20. Teenage parents are less likely to complete school and more likely to end up on welfare than nonchildbearing teens. The children of teenage parents tend to have less supportive home environments, more behavioral problems, and poorer health.[8]

In addition to teenage pregnancy and the social and economic problems that are perceived to stem from it, proponents of abstinence-only education cite other recurring concerns: abortion, STDs (sexually transmitted diseases), AIDS and the coercion of young adults into sexual behaviour that they are not ready for by their peers. Related issues, which are articulated mainly by religious and/or right-wing groups, are to do with what are felt to be core moral values, especially the central importance of the family and of heterosexual marriage as the only legitimate context for sexual activity. The Medical Institute for Sexual Health states: 'Science clearly shows that the behavior choices necessary for optimal health are sexual abstinence for unmarried inviduals and faithfulness in marriage' – which is why they are concerned to promote 'the preservation of the family as the center of our society'.[9] Or, as a UK-based online Christian magazine puts it: 'Sex is meant to be enjoyed in a secure and loving relationship. No relationship is secure outside the public commitment of marriage.'[10] This site goes on to list '8 reasons why sex outside marriage is harmful', which overlap to a large extent with those held by abstinence-education supporters: '(1) Sexually transmitted diseases can be caught; (2) A baby may result; (3) Most people prefer new things to second-hand things; (4) Casual sex takes the trust out of our future marriage; (5) Casual sex is a lie; (6) Casual sex can cause depressions; (7) Concentrating on sex can spoil or even prevent a friendship; (8) God has a better plan'.[11] As one article outlines, the 'constant targets' of abstinence-only promoters are 'sexuality education curriculum [sic] that include information on contraception; programs or materials that mention lesbian, gay, bisexual, transgender, or questioning . . . individuals; books or videos deemed "sexually explicit;" and organizations such as Planned Parenthood that provide medically accurate sexuality education to many school districts across the country'.[12]

While similar stories concerning teenage sex are emerging in Britain – research on British teen sexual behaviour carried out by the Trust for the Study of Adolescence reveals a high level of ignorance and risky sexual behaviour among teens – this has led to widespread calls not for abstinence education, but for *more* comprehensive sex education that will also address emotional issues, such as peer pressure.[13] This call was 'backed by *CosmoGIRL* magazine' with a campaign that puns playfully on the abstinence-only message, highlighting the difference of approach: 'Just say Know campaign'.[14] The Know/No pun, which refers to the 'Just Say No' campaign to discourage children from using recreational drugs, captures the two approaches to the sex education conundrum, which in the US are often set against one another: knowledge and abstinence.

On the surface, the debate over abstinence-only education is often portrayed as yet another manifestation of the so-called 'culture wars' raging in the US, with the religious Right pitted against left-wing secular progressives. There is certainly evidence to support this view, and it is undeniable that the tone of the debate is never less than passionate.[15] What such a reading of the situation obscures, however, is that there appears to be a general concern about teen sexuality that blurs political or religious boundaries – at least when parents' opinions are being surveyed. It also seems that the appeal to 'values' has unsettled traditional voting constituencies, with traditionally Democrat voters voting Republican because they want such issues to be addressed. In addition, some of the terms central to this debate – such as 'evangelical' – are themselves problematic, in this instance because it suggests an undifferentiated bloc which does not exist as such.[16] And, while many parents are keen to have abstinence as part of a sex-education curriculum, most do not seem to want it to be the *only* information their child receives. Nonetheless, abstinence education in one form or another is what most of their children will now experience.

Birth of a movement

In 2003, Martha E. Kempner summarized the increasing prominence of abstinence education over the previous decade:

> There has been a dramatic rise in the amount of money that both federal and state governments spend on abstinence-only-until-marriage programs; the current administration is

committed to increasing funding; the media has seized on the concept of the 'new virginity'; and communities have welcomed abstinence-only speakers, fear-based curricula, and chastity rallies into their school with nary a second thought.[17]

In fact this process has not been quite so smooth. A recent report states that the Sex Information and Education Council of the United States (SIECUS) 'tracked 153 controversies in 38 states in the 2004–05 school year', in which '[p]arents, students, school board members, supportive organizations, and public health professionals have all furthered the cause of comprehensive sexuality education'.[18]

The 'chastity' movement emerged in 1981, when Jeremiah Denton, the Baptist Republican senator for Alabama, targeted abortion and teenage sex with his Adolescent Family Life Act (AFLA) by 'promot[ing] self-discipline and other prudent approaches'.[19] Though initially ridiculed or ignored, this movement gained momentum and, '[t]wenty years later, the Right has all but won the sex-education wars. In 1997, the US Congress committed a quarter billion dollars over five years' time to finance more education in chastity, whose name had been replaced by the less churchy, more twelve-steppish, *abstinence*.'[20]

It was not just the Republicans who encouraged abstinence education; President Clinton is thought by some commentators to have supported it in 1994, with his '$400 million campaign against teenage pregnancy [which] turned "virginity into a matter of public health, not just private morality"'.[21] In 2004, SIECUS could report that 'the government currently spends nearly $138 million per year for abstinence-only-until-marriage programs', and this despite the evidence from numerous national surveys that demonstrate 'overwhelming support for a comprehensive approach to sexuality education'.[22] In 2004, a commission looking into the quality of the most widely used abstinence curricula found that of the thirteen surveyed, eleven contained numerous instances of 'false, misleading, or distorted information'. Only two were considered 'accurate'. The congressional staff analysis, drawn up by Henry A. Waxman, criticized the curricula for including 'unproved claims, subjective conclusions or outright falsehoods regarding reproductive health, gender traits and when life begins'.[23] Since 2005, the figure dedicated to abstinence education has risen to nearly $170 million per annum – which is less than President Bush had wanted.[24]

Some commentators place a proportion of the blame for the success of abstinence-only programmes on the apathy of promoters of comprehensive sex education. Judith Levine, for instance, argues that nobody was hugely exercised about it, that it was a 'political backwater' that 'hardly anyone paid attention to'. This meant that there was 'no national movement, no coherent cultural-political agenda' to support and promote comprehensive sex education in the face of its opponents.[25] Nonetheless, economics clearly plays an important role in deciding which sex education programme a school chooses to adopt. As Kempner points out, 'as the economy falters and school systems suffer from a lack of resources, fully funded programs become even more appealing'.[26] The lure of financial support was effective and many public schools succumbed. Even those who supported and promoted comprehensive sex education could not ultimately resist the force of the abstinence tide: organizations such as the Planned Parenthood Federation, Advocates for Youth and SIECUS publicly spoke out about their support for abstinence as part of sex education, and '[t]oday comprehensive sexuality education calls itself abstinence-plus education'.[27]

Many of the sources confirm the impression of a split between health-care professionals and religious groups: while the two groups seem to agree that the question should be addressed, they have very different ideas as to how that should happen. While those who support comprehensive sex education claim that it allows adolescents to make informed choices, proponents of abstinence education argue that such information in fact encourages young people to have sex earlier.[28] Maintaining virginity, for abstinence supporters, is not only about health (and economic) benefits, but also about emotional and moral benefits: guilt, jealousy, depression are just some of the alleged psychological side-effects of casual or pre-marital sex. In contrast, virginity loss *within* marriage is presented as a genuine, wonderful, beautiful and romantic experience – inevitably so, as one has waited to build an emotional relationship that involves trust and love with one's partner: 'Only marry your best friend! Sex can follow, beautifully and easily, if the friendship and caring are there first.'[29]

There is some suggestion that the word 'abstinence' itself was taken 'from the hugely popular movement of twelve-step anti-"addiction" programs based on the model of Alcoholics Anonymous, which preached that only complete renunciation and daily recommitment could bring a bad habit under control'.[30] Certainly, casual sex is referred to by abstinence-only supporters as 'addictive', potentially as devastating in its consequences (physical, physiological, economic) as a drug addiction. They also suggest that sex is dangerous, which has led to their critics accusing them of promoting not sex *education*, but using solely fear- and shame-based tactics to scare teenagers into maintaining their virginity: '[T]hese programs typically omit critical information, contain medical misinformation, include sexist and anti-choice bias and often have a foundation in fundamentalist religious beliefs.'[31] The position of abstinence-only proponents, when not couched in religious terms, is, as stated above, that comprehensive sex education actually encourages young people to have sex.[32]

Yet it appears that the approach of at least some abstinence-only curricula has changed over the years. While initial 'drafts of fear-based abstinence-only-until-marriage curricula were clearly religious in nature and made outrageous and dangerous suggestions like washing one's genitals with Lysol after sexual activity', this has shifted to a replacement of 'overt religious statements' with 'subtle references to spirituality and morality while blatantly false information has been replaced with mild exaggerations based on legitimate sources'.[33] Nonetheless, Waxman's 2004 report suggests that problems are ongoing.

Rather than moral concerns, others highlight the economic and race-political considerations that they see underlying governmental support for abstinence education. Chris Mayo, for instance, argues that in the 1990s, 'abstinence education became a centerpiece in the war against welfare':

Included in drafts of the [welfare reform] act are an array of statistics pointing to the link between single motherhood and poverty, the rising rate of illegitimacy among black Americans, rates of black male criminal activity among young men raised by single mothers, and the rate of criminal activity in neighborhoods with a greater incidence of single parent households.[34]

There are wider social issues at stake in this debate. Mayo points out that, '[r]ather than focusing concern on the relationship between poverty *per se* and criminal activity, these statements link single motherhood, and also female sexual activity, with criminality and social decay'.[35] This is not a new story. Yet part of what arguably makes abstinence so attractive to US governments is the long and pervasive – though complex – history of Puritan attitudes to the management of the self and its emphasis on self-control. In this world-view, avoiding 'sin' is down to individual will; it is the will that must be trained or educated into moral behaviour.[36] This became increasingly the responsibility of women, who, as 'Moral Mothers' would pass on the right values to their children.[37] In fact, sex education in the US was brought into school curricula in the late nineteenth century by an organization called 'The Mother's Crusade' which, taking 'child rearing ideas and theories of sex education from social purists', argued that the ideal citizen they envisaged as shaping the nation needed to learn and internalize 'purity values'. Purity reformers acknowledged poverty as a powerful shaper of the individual's life, but were torn between this and their belief that resulting criminality or prostitution were to be read as signs of 'delinquency or criminality'.[38] Prostitutes should be rehabilitated, but emphasis was laid on the individual's responsibility, rather than on prevailing social conditions and economic factors. This legacy is evident in the welfare reform act that Mayo refers to, the 'Personal Responsibility and Work Opportunity Reconciliation Act of 1996', to which abstinence education was central. Some commentators see a close interrelation between nineteenth-century and contemporary purity movements, with their shared emphasis on traditional ideas concerning the centrality of the family, the clear division of gender roles and the emphasis on individual responsibility. To critics, the thrust of such ideals and policies is an attempt to impose a set of norms onto a diverse and complex populace, effectively stigmatizing those who do not fit its narrowly defined categories.

Virginity promotion through abstinence education thus intersects with questions of social regulation on a number of levels. Within the family, the question of control is closely related to how parents feel about their children being sexually active and autonomous. Abstinence-education supporters repeatedly cite the negative influence of peer groups and a wider culture that commodifies and glamorizes sex as eroding the influence of parents on their adolescents' behaviour. Some supporters of comprehensive sex education share this concern, and think that abstinence can be a valuable component in sex education when defined as freedom to resist pressure to have sex. Others counter that parents who support abstinence education are doing so because they find it difficult to acknowledge the separate individuality of their 'child': 'In this sense, abstinence is about reversing, or at least holding back, the coming of age, which for parents is a story of loss, as their children establish passionate connections with people and values outside the family.'[39] The argument here is that adults *cannot* in the end be actively involved in their teenager's sexual initiation, as it is an experience that by its very definition excludes the parent(s), and that means accepting certain risks and trying to prepare the adolescent for these with correct information on sexual and emotional health. To insist on abstinence is therefore not only to treat young adults patronizingly, but also to try to prevent their independent growth, to arrest their development at an imagined pre-sexual state of innocence.

Abstinence tomorrow?

Reports on the effect of abstinence-only education seem to suggest that it does influence teen sexual behaviour, though not in ways that clearly support either side in the debate. As one article states, the findings on how effective virginity or abstinence pledges made by adolescents were in preventing or postponing sexual activity did not offer a definitive answer.[40] Results published in a January 2001 issue of the *American Journal of Sociology* 'were mixed, offering ammunition for either abstinence-only or comprehensive sex education proponents, depending on which findings were emphasized'. Some of these findings were as follows:

- Pledgers began sexual activity on average 18 months later than non-pledgers.
- Pledging had little effect among older teens (18 and older).
- The vow was effective only in environments where fewer than 30 per cent of a school's students were pledgers, thus allowing pledgers to form identities unique from the majority of other students.
- Among those teens who eventually did have intercourse, pledgers were less likely to use contraception than non-pledgers.[41]

However, findings in 2005 were less optimistic. One six-year study of adolescent sexual behaviour examined it in relation to familial, educational and religious contexts. Its results suggest that those adolescents whose parents disapproved strongly of sexual relationships, as well as those with higher grades at school, were less likely to have contracted STIs (sexually transmitted infections) six years later. On the other hand, '[f]eelings of connection to family or school, reported importance of religion, attending a parochial school and pledges of virginity during adolescence did not predict STI status six years later.'[42]

It is a point worth making that what people think about the validity of abstinence-only education depends to a considerable extent on where they get their information from, particularly if they rely heavily on such sources as television and newspapers. Reporting on newspaper coverage of virginity pledges in American newspapers from 1987 to 2001, one study shows that many tended to foreground its positive aspects rather than providing a balanced picture: '[G]iven the comparatively small number of articles that included any arguments in opposition to virginity pledges, it was apparent that stories about virginity pledge programs tended to favor supportive messages and generally were not balanced with public health arguments, evidence-based skepticism, or public policy implications.' The study raises the critical issue that the proponents of evidence-based sex education 'often overlook the power of news organizations to shape attitudes, beliefs, and policies'. Because of this, the information they want to convey to the public is not always put across in an effective way, weakening their chances of gaining public support.[43]

Some commentators in America point out that the issue of abstinence education is not one that those in the rest of the world should feel – smugly or sadly – distant from. They note that the political and religious groups lobbying for abstinence education are powerful, and are not content with influencing only national policy: '[M]any people do not realize how influential these very same groups have become in the international arena. They are playing an ever-increasing role in countries and regions as diverse as Africa, Asia, and both western and eastern Europe.' What they want to see happening in these countries is a replication of what has been implemented in the US: 'Their primary goals remain the same: promoting the "traditional family," instituting abstinence-only-until-marriage programs, redirecting HIV/AIDS education, and limiting access to family planning resources and abortion.'[44] This, their critics maintain, is achieved by a combination of tactics: 'challenging international agreements on and restricting US funding' for programmes that do not share their agenda. So far, they have been successful. The American government's five-year 'President's Emergency Plan for AIDS Relief', formulated in 2004, makes available $133 million every year to 'abstinence-until-marriage programs in focus countries in Africa and the Caribbean'.[45] The impact of these policies – feared by many who work in the sector to be, at best, counterproductive – will no doubt become clearer in the next years.

What remains conspicuously absent in many of these discussions is any definition of what, precisely, constitutes maintained virginity or abstinence. Is one to abstain from penetrative heterosexual intercourse? What about anal intercourse or oral sex? Laura Carpenter argues that '[I]n contemporary popular and academic literature, the term virginity loss denotes first coitus'; and not only first coitus, but mainly first coitus in relation to 'vaginal intercourse'.[46] Yet young adults do not always agree on that definition.[47] In a study of how different individuals defined their own loss of virginity, the intricacies and complexities in the ways people think about virginity and its loss are revealed, showing that 'beliefs and behaviors vary meaningfully across and within gender and sexual orientation'. This is something not frequently addressed or even acknowledged by abstinence-only-until-marriage proponents. Interviewees also differed in their views on whether they thought anal sex counted as loss of virginity, or oral sex, or whether rape constituted a loss of virginity.[48] Age also mattered, with 'younger respondents ... more likely than their older counterparts to view same-sex virginity loss as possible' and to 'exclude rape from their definitions of virginity'. The study concludes that 'younger respondents appear to be redefining virginity loss rather than choosing to abandon the concept of virginity altogether'.[49]

Some contemporary advice books aimed at teenagers do take account of this shift. *Everything You Need to Know About Virginity*, for instance, says that '[a]nyone who has never had sex – whether a guy or a girl, gay or straight – can be considered a virgin'.[50] This book also notes the increasing interest in virginity in the US and lists some myths about virginity, including the one that waiting until marriage guarantees a pleasurable experience. In its approach to virginity, it demonstrates an uneasy tightrope walk between providing accurate information for teenagers while not neglecting a 'values' approach. It is interesting to note that virginity is a topic for the 'Need to Know Library' series, alongside other titles such as, 'AIDS', 'Alcohol', 'Anger', 'Drug Addiction', 'Eating Disorders', 'Growing Up Female', 'Incest', 'Teen Suicide', 'Smoking', 'Stress', 'Protecting Yourself and Others From Abduction'. Is virginity a 'problem' topic comparable to these others? What do these titles say about the fears surrounding adolescence in Western society?

Perhaps, like virginity, adolescence also crystallizes some of the fundamental issues that trouble a given society at a particular time. Like virginity, it is perceived as a transitional period, a threshold to adulthood. Like the virgin, the adolescent is therefore also an unknown, and unpredictable. It is in this struggle over teen sexuality that virginity has re-emerged most visibly from margins to which it was never fully relegated. It is worth remembering for the future that, while virginity can mean many things, those meanings have never been innocent.

Notes

All translations from the Middle English are my own, unless otherwise stated. I have silently modernized spellings in quotations throughout – A.B.

Preface

1   Kelly, *Performing Virginity*, p. 121.

Chapter 1: 'I Don't Know Virgin'

1   The chapter title is taken from Broumas and Begley, 'I Don't Know Virgin'. Epigraph from Fogel and Lauver, eds., *Sexual Health Promotion*, p. 43. The rest of the definition reads: 'This membrane is normally perforated to allow for menses. The hymen is visualized as an irregular narrow fold around the introitus, forming a hymenal ring. The hymen serves no physiological purpose but over the years has taken on considerable emotional and cultural significance. According to myth, women who possess an intact hymen are sexually inexperienced or virginal, while those whose hymens are torn are non-virginal. This idea is not true; the hymen can be broken by vigorous exercise or remain intact even with sexual intercourse.' For a popular online resource that addresses young adults in a jocular tone, see 'The Hymen', at <http://www.rotten.com/library/sex/hymen/>.

2   Underhill and Dewhurst, 'The Doctor Cannot Always Tell', p. 375.

Virgins

3   On the role of the hymen in the development of gynaecological exami-
    nations in the nineteenth and twentieth centuries, see Brumberg, *The
    Body Project*, pp. 145–53.

4   See Kelly, *Performing Virginity*, pp. 25–8.

5   See Cadden, *Meanings*, esp. pp. 3–4.

6   See Dixon, *Perilous Chastity*, pp. 20 ff.

7   See Kelly, *Performing Virginity*, p. 25.

8   See Kelly, 'Menaced Masculinity', p. 104.

9   Cited in Jacquart and Thomasset, *Sexuality*, p. 44.

10 Sharp, *The Midwives Book*, pp. 48, 50.

11 Crooke, *Mikrokosmographia*, p. 235.

12 Weld, 'Concerning the Proofs of Virginity', p. 55.

13 Astruc, *A Treatise on the Diseases of Women*, I, pp. 121–2.

14 Beck, *Elements*, I, p. 73; emphasis in the original. He then goes on to list
    names of those who argue for and against the hymen's existence.

15 Venette, 'Chap. IV', p. 86.

16 Beck, *Elements*, I, p. 78. He is here referring specifically to the medical
    examiner's role in cases of alleged rape. Brumberg notes that while doc-
    tors in nineteenth-century North America 'readily agreed that the hymen
    was an unreliable indicator', they still 'got involved in policing the private
    parts of American girls' and were 'frequently called upon to provide sci-
    entific testimony about the condition of the membrane' (*The Body
    Project*, p. 150).

17 See Merritt, 'Vulvar and Genital Trauma'.

18 Lemay, ed. and trans., *Women's Secrets*, p. 128.

19 Ibid., p. 127.

20 See Cadden, 'Western Medicine', p. 66.

21 Lemay, ed. and trans., *Women's Secrets*, p. 127.

22 See Kelly, *Performing Virginity*, pp, 23–9.

23 See ibid., p. 23.

24 Sharp, *The Midwives Book*, p. 42.

25 Venette, 'Chap. IV', pp. 88, 89. Boucé notes that Venette's work was
    'reprinted well into the twentieth century, and translated into most
    European languages' ('Some Sexual Beliefs', p. 30).

26 Paris, *Medical Jurisprudence*, I, p. 429, note (*a*). Paris is dismissive about
    such 'proofs' of defloration; nonetheless, his mention of them shows their
    longevity.

27 Lemay, ed. and trans., *Women's Secrets*, p. 128.

Notes

28   Weld, 'Concerning the Proofs of Virginity', pp. 49, 46.

29   Venette, 'Chap. IV', pp. 86–7.

30   Dixon, *Perilous Chastity*, p. 11 and Cadden, *Meanings*, p. 17.

31   Kelly, *Performing Virginity*, p. 22.

32   Lemay, ed. and trans, *Women's Secrets*, pp. 129, 96.

33   Jacquart and Thomasset, *Sexuality*, p. 174.

34   See ibid., pp. 75, 191.

35   See, for instance, Dixon, *Perilous Chastity*, p. 6.

36   Dixon, *Perilous Chastity*, p. 223.

37   Ibid., p. 15.

38   See Lemay, 'Introduction', in *Women's Secrets*, pp. 1–58 (p. 5).

39   King, *Disease of Virgins*, p. 50.

40   *Aristotle's Compleat and Experience'd Midwife*, p. 158.

41   Ibid., p. 159.

42   Cited in Dixon, *Perilous Chastity*, p. 44.

43   See McFarland, 'The Rhetoric of Medicine', in which he attributes the illness's 'classic' description to Johannes Lange, 'physician to the Electors of the Palatinate' (p. 250).

44   King, *Disease of Virgins*, p. 67.

45   Culpeper, in *The Idea of Practical Physick* (London, 1657), adds that the illness not only turns the girl's face a shade of green, but also manifests itself in headaches, respiratory problems, fever, an upset stomach and palpitations.

46   As Dixon states, 'In both eras chlorosis was said to occur primarily in adolescent girls, and the symptoms – weakness, fainting, difficulty in breathing, appetite disorders, erratic pulse, pallor, and mental disturbances – were identical' (*Perilous Chastity*, pp. 239–40; see also King, *Disease of Virgins*).

47   See Dixon, *Perilous Chastity*, p. 47.

48   Whytt, *Observations*, p. 103. See also Dixon, *Perilous Chastity*, pp. 223–4.

49   Ibid., p. 104.

50   See Dixon, *Perilous Chastity*, p. 238.

51   See Cadden, 'Western Medicine', p. 62, and Lemay, ed. and trans., *Women's Secrets*, Ch. IX, comm. B, p. 127; see also p. 70.

52   Cadden, *Meanings*, p. 276.

53   Cited in Cadden, 'Western Medicine', p. 59.

54   See Kelly, *Performing Virginity*, pp. 23–4; Cadden, *Meanings*, pp. 273–4.

55   Crooke, *Mikrokosmographia*, p. 238.

56   Sharp, *The Midwives Book*, p. 45.

57   See Ambrose Paré, cited in Dixon, *Perilous Chastity*, p. 45.

58   See Haller and Haller, *The Physician and Sexuality*.

59   See ibid., pp. 76ff.

60   Otto Juettner, 'The Place of Women in the Modern Business World as Affecting the Future of the Race', *Bulletin*, American Academy of Medicine, 9 (1908), 351, cited in Haller and Haller, *The Physician and Sexuality*, p. 79.

61   Coley, 'On Imperforate Hymen'.

62   Davies, 'Syphilis'.

63   Beale, 'Labour', p. 98.

64   Ibid., p. 68.

65   Freud, 'The Taboo of Virginity', p. 205.

66   Ibid., p. 206.

67   See Merritt, 'Vulvar and Genital Trauma'.

68   Carpenter, 'Gender', p. 345.

69   See Dixon, *Perilous Chastity*, p. 15.

70   While there is a serious debate to be had about whether doctors who help women to present themselves as physically intact are helping the women, or are in fact helping to prolong the idea that physical virginity is ascertainable, these cosmetic surgery clinics are mainly concerned with 'selling' virginity as a product.

71   See Brumberg, *The Body Project*, pp. 158–60.

72   Website, Atlanta Center for Laparoscopic Urogynecology: <http://urogynecologychannel.net>. My emphasis.

73   Website, Liberty Women's Health Care: <http://www.libertywomenshealth.com/9.html>. Emphasis in the original.

74   While some of the procedures are designed to help women suffering from a range of medical conditions, such as injuries to the genitalia caused by childbirth, I am referring to procedures that are sold for purely aesthetic reasons.

75   Website, Liberty Women's Health Care.

76   For practice of hymenoplasty in other countries (with a Christian cultural background), see, for instance, Roberts, 'Reconstructing Virginity'. Here, Roberts cites experts who challenge the claim that 'hymen repair' surgery is straightforward and 'a small price to pay' for women who fear the ostracization that loss of virginity will bring: 'Operations to reconstruct

Notes

women's hymens are costly (up to US $1000), provide no health benefit, and run the risk of serious medical complications, says Miriam Bethancourt, of the Association of Guatemalan Gynaecologists and Obstetricians. She is highly critical of the "unscrupulous doctors" who, she says, are exploiting societal pressure and doing unnecessary operations. Bethancourt believes that most of the surgeons who do these operations have not completed the full necessary medical training ... Women repeatedly testify that they are not informed of any potential risks or side-effects of the procedures.' On the 2005 banning of virginity testing in South Africa, which had faced a revival in the 1990s, see Vincent, 'Virginity Testing'; on coercive uses of virginity tests, see also Parla, 'The "Honor" of the State'.

77 On the debate between medical professionals over the practice of hymenoplasty, see the section entitled 'Ethical Dilemma: Should Doctors Reconstruct the Vaginal Introitus of Adolescent Girls to Mimic the Virginal State?', in *British Medical Journal*, 316.7129 (February 1998), 459–62.

78 For such surgical services see, for instance, also <http://medpages.obgyn. net/docdetail.cfm?sn=23751>. These issues have been covered in a wide range of women's magazines. One clinic demonstrates its expertise and the importance of such surgical procedures by having a page on its website listing all the magazines featuring articles on this topic, including, among many others, *Bazaar*, *Cosmopolitan*, *Marie Claire* and *Elle* (see <http://www.drmatlock.com/media.htm>).

79 Cited in Dannenfeldt, 'Egyptian Mumia', p. 165.

80 See Dannenfeldt, 'Egyptian Mumia', p. 174.

Chapter 2: 'The World's Redemption'

1 Anon., *Holy Maidenhood*, p. 228.

2 Venette, 'Chap. IV', p. 85.

3 Anon., *Holy Maidenhood*, p. 240.

4 Ibid., p. 231.

5 Anon., *Ancrene Wisse*, p. 100.

6 While not as much research has been done on the role of virginity in the middle and lower social orders, there is evidence to suggest that it remained important, especially in relation to power and money. See Phillips, 'Four Virgins' Tales'.

Virgins

7   For more on this, see Elliott, *Fallen Bodies*.
8   Elliott, *Fallen Bodies*, p. 83.
9   Ibid., p. 82.
10 St Jerome, 'Commentatorium in Epistolam ad Ephesios'; trans. by and cited in Oppel, 'Saint Jerome', 21.
11 In addition, virginity was not important for men in the secular sphere, although it remained so for women.
12 Aelred of Rievaulx, 'The Nun of Watton', p. 454.
13 Ibid., pp. 454–5.
14 Elkins, *Holy Women*, p. 111.
15 Bertrams, *Celibacy*, p. 7.
16 Ibid., pp. 16–17.
17 Ibid., pp. 8, 20–21.
18 Thurian, *Marriage and Celibacy*, pp. 45–6.
19 Ibid., p. 49.
20 Bertrams, *Celibacy*, pp. 24–5.
21 Anon., *Holy Maidenhood*, p. 232.
22 Ibid., pp. 236–9.
23 *The Life of Christina of Markyate*, p. 59.
24 See Bernau, 'Gender and Sexuality'.
25 Bertrams, *Celibacy*, p. 21.
26 Tertullian, 'On the Veiling of Virgins', IV, p. 31.
27 See Henry, 'Mystery of Virginity', p. 79.
28 Ibid., p. 88.
29 Ibid., pp. 89–90.
30 Ibid., p. 91.
31 Ibid., pp. 95, 84.
32 Luther, 'The Estate of Marriage', p. 135.
33 See Hackett, *Virgin Mother*.
34 See Hackett, *Virgin Mother*, pp. 204–5.
35 Shinners, ed., *Medieval Popular Religion*, pp. 113, 115, 116. See also Phillips, *Medieval Maidens*, esp. chap. 5; and Warner, *Alone of All Her Sex*.
36 St Ambrose, 'Concerning Virgins'.
37 Luther, 'The Estate of Marriage', pp. 136, 137–8.
38 Cited in Thurian, *Marriage and Celibacy*, p. 21.
39 Waterworth, ed. and trans., *The Council of Trent*, p. 195.
40 See Leites, *Puritan Conscience*, p. 11.

Notes

41   Hackett, *Virgin Mother*, p. 123.

42   Bentley, *The Fift Lampe of Virginitie*.

43   Rogers, 'Enclosure of Virginity', pp. 229, 238, 239. See also Taylor, *Holy Living*, esp. p. 74.

44   Rogers, 'Enclosure of Virginity', pp. 240, 242.

45   Winstanley, *Fire in the Bush*, pp. 50–51.

46   Anon., *A Looking-Glasse*, pp. 16–17.

47   Ibid., pp. 19–22; emphasis mine.

48   See Leites, *Puritan Conscience*, esp. p. 11.

49   Morey, *Religion and Sexuality*, p. 2.

50   Foster, *Religion and Sexuality*, pp. 26–7, 6.

51   See ibid., esp. pp. 229, 234.

52   See Clark and Richardson, eds., *Women and Religion*, p. 162.

53   Avery, *Sketches*, pp. 9, 18, 22.

54   Pelham, 'A Shaker's Answer', pp. 31, 33, 36–7.

55   See Leites, *Puritan Conscience*, esp. pp. 16, 17–18, 234.

56   For more on this, see Haller and Haller, *The Physician*, p. xii.

57   See Davies and Loughlin, eds., *Sex These Days*.

58   Smith, *Christian America?*, p. 1. Smith adds in footnote 1 that: 'Scholars generally agree that conservative Protestants represent about 25 to 30 percent of the American population. Narrow measurements based on religious self-identification reveal smaller numbers, while those based on broad theological beliefs can yield much larger numbers'.

59   Wilson, 'Foreword'.

60   The term 'conservative evangelical' covers a wide range of different and diverse groups and should not be taken to indicate an absolutely homogenous group, even while their views concerning sex and premarital virginity do not vary much.

61   Elliot, *Passion and Purity*, pp. 22, 130–32.

62   Stephens, *A Passion for Purity*, pp. xiii, 2–4, 7.

63   Elliot, *Passion and Purity*, pp. 14, 68–9, 85.

64   Harris, *I Kissed Dating Goodbye*, p. 15.

65   Ibid., pp. 21, 93–4, 36.

66   As Elliot puts it, '[W]hen you get to the point where you can't keep your hands off each other, it's time to get married. The current "touchy-poo" brand of Christianity had no place in Paul's thinking' (*Passion and Purity*, pp. 93–4).

67   Harris, *I Kissed Dating Goodbye*, pp. 43, 46, 71, 53–4, 88.

68 Ibid., pp. 90, 91, 117.

69 Ibid., pp. 141, 62, 66–7, 77, 78.

70 Stephens, *A Passion for Purity*, p. 5. In Stephens's case, this might not be so surprising: the head of the World Changers Church International, Dr Creflo Dollar, promotes a 'prosperity oriented' teaching that has attracted criticism.

71 Harris, *I Kissed Dating Goodbye*, pp. 159, 60

72 *Revolve: The Complete New Testament*, pp. 21, 208. Harris also makes this point: 'Scripture plainly states that a Christian should not even consider a non-Christian for a spouse. "Don't team up with those who are unbelievers," the Bible says (2 Corinthians 6:14).' *I Kissed Dating Goodbye*, p. 177; Harris is here citing from *Holy Bible*, New Living Translation (1993).

73 *Revolve: The Complete New Testament*, p. 255, 21, 77; *Revolve 2: The Complete New Testament*, p. 224.

74 Elliot, *Passion and Purity*, pp. 33, 146.

75 Harris, *I Kissed Dating Goodbye*, pp. 98–9.

76 Ibid., p. 146.

77 *Revolve*, p. 255.

78 Harris, *I Kissed Dating Goodbye*, p. 79.

79 Nilsen, 'Virginity', p. 6. See also Bernau, 'Girls on Film'.

80 See 'Secondary/ "Renewed" Virginity', at <http://www.geocities.com/the-virginclub/Secondary.htm?200611>. This site also includes links to other websites dealing with secondary virginity.

81 Greg and Smalley, 'A Renewed Virginity'.

82 *Revolve 2*, p. 80.

Chapter 3: 'An Unknown Alphabet'

1 Munich, 'What Lily Knew', pp. 144–5.

2 Cowley, 'Maidenhead', l. 29.

3 Kelly, *Performing Virginity*, p. 139.

4 See Peek, 'King by Day'.

5 Shohet, 'Figuring Chastity', p. 148.

6 Ingram, 'VII. The Interpreters', l. 6.

7 Shohet, 'Figuring Chastity', p. 148.

8 Holmes, 'To a Blank Sheet of Paper', ll. 1–4.

9 'Ephelia', 'Maidenhead', p. 278.

10 Guillaume de Lorris and Jean de Meun, *The Romance of the Rose*.

Notes

11 Ibid., pp. 302–3.

12 Innes, trans. and intro., *The Metamorphoses*, Bk. X, pp. 231–2.

13 It is therefore perhaps inevitable that Pygmalion's grandson, King Cinyras, ends up committing incest with his daughter, Myrrha, mimicking the logic of Pygmalion's love for his creation.

14 Shakespeare, *A Midsummer Night's Dream*, I.i.46–51.

15 Porter, *The Sheikh's Virgin*, pp. 6, 100. 'Baraka' is a Middle Eastern country invented by the author, who describes it as a 'mix of cultures – Berber, Bedouin, Arab and European', whose women 'were still protected, sheltered, segregated' (p. 10).

16 Marton, *The Disobedient Virgin*, pp. 10, 112.

17 Monroe, *The Greek's Innocent Virgin*, pp. 81, 83.

18 Shakespeare, *A Midsummer Night's Dream*, I.i.28–32.

19 Ayres, 'Emb. 9. Love a Ticklish Game'; emphasis mine.

20 Holmes, 'To a Blank Sheet of Paper', ll. 21–8.

21 Herrick, 'To the Virgins', ll. 1, 13–16.

22 Marvell, 'To His Coy Mistress', ll. 27–30.

23 Guillaume de Lorris and Jean de Meun, *The Romance of the Rose*, p. 330.

24 Heyrick, 'Advice to a Virgin', ll. 4–7, 13–19.

25 Hill, 'Advice to the Virgins', ll. 28–30, 41–2.

26 Fordyce, 'Sermon IV: On Female Virtue', pp. 176–7.

27 Tate, 'The Virgin', ll. 4, 8.

28 See Bernau, '"Saint, Witch, Man, Maid or Whore?"', pp. 218–19.

29 Porter, *The Sheikh's Virgin*, p. 136.

30 Duganne, 'The Three Maries', l. 8.

31 Dolben, 'Pro Castitate'.

32 Stephens, *Virgin for Sale*, p. 31.

33 See Sturges, 'The Pardoner', p. 272.

34 Taylor, 'Reading the Dirty Bits', p. 282.

35 Clare, 'A Maiden-Haid', l. 4.

36 Marton, *The Disobedient Virgin*, pp. 50–51, 71.

37 Tate, 'The Virgin', ll. 14, 27–30.

38 Mandeville, *The Virgin Unmask'd*, p. 19.

39 Kendall, 'X. Female Beauty', ll. 1–2, 7–10, 18, 21–6, 20, 24.

40 Kendall's poem is also rather disingenuous concerning virginity's 'naturalness'. The elves and fairies that make the virgin might be 'along by nature led' (l. 5), but they also 'refine', 'steep', steal' and 'snatch' from nature in order to create her – all processes that suggest craft and artifice.

41 Heyrick, 'Advice to a Virgin', ll. 20–22, 34–5, 28–31. Examples of virgins who are so completely chaste that they do not arouse desire despite their beauty are rare in literature but do exist. These women (like the Virgin Mary or Diana, the virgin goddess) have an exceptional status. See, for instance, Edmund Spenser's description of Belphoebe in *The Faerie Queene*.

42 Chaucer, 'The Physician's Tale', ll. 43, 51, 248–9.

43 See Bloch, *Medieval Misogyny*, esp. pp. 93–112.

44 Brian, *The V Club*, pp. 195, 27, 94, 196, 103, 105, 34, 139, 236.

45 *The N-Town Play*. All the plays referred to here are in Volume I, and are cited with reference to their numerical place in the volume, followed by line number: 12. 27, 30; 14. 174; 15. 150–54, 206–7, 256.

46 Petroff, *Body and Soul*, p. 26.

47 Brundage, *Law, Sex*, p. 427.

48 Poos, 'Sex, Lies', 594–5.

49 See Kelly, *Performing Virginity*, p. 63.

50 The latter is represented beautifully in the Lady and the Unicorn tapestries housed in the Musée National du Moyen Age in Paris.

51 A different approach is taken in the unexpectedly successful film, *The Forty-Year-Old Virgin* (2005). Here, the virgin of the title, Andy, takes his girlfriend's teenage daughter, Marla, to a sexual health clinic. In a group discussion of adults and their teen offspring, it emerges that Marla is still a virgin, something the rest of the group – her peers and their parents alike – find laughable. Nonetheless, the film still distinguishes between 'nice' women and 'trashy' women, a distinction that is made on the basis of how sexually available the woman in question is.

52 Middleton and Rowley, *The Changeling*, III. iv. 142–4, IV. ii. 149–50.

53 Guillaume de Loris and Jean de Meun, *The Romance of the Rose*, p. 333.

54 Blume, *Forever*, pp. 89–90. The stark opposition between an idealized first sexual encounter and the sordid 'reality' of college campus sex is narrated vividly in Ellis's *Rules of Attraction*, pp. 13–16.

55 Cleland, *Fanny Hill*, pp. 59, 98.

56 Smith, *Chasing Amy*, p. 228.

57 Anon., 'The Loving Chamber-Maid', stanza 14. The song is subtitled: 'Being the Art to lie with a Man and yet be a Virgin'.

58 Anon., 'The Country Miss', stanza 2.

59 While Telly's obsession with very young virgins is clearly also meant to reflect his own isolation and a wider social malaise, his opinion that virgins

are safe because they have no diseases is based on more than just 'common sense'. The bitter irony is that he is the one infected with HIV. Today, the myth that raping or having sex with a virgin can cure a man of AIDS has gained worldwide currency, with tragic consequences.

60   The film was also released under the title *American Virgin* (2000).

61   Shakespeare and Fletcher, *Two Noble Kinsmen*, 'Prologue', ll. 1–3.

62   Shakespeare, *The Tempest*, IV.i.13–14.

63   Barker, 'A Virgin Life', ll. 1–2, 4, 9–10, 36.

64   Cavendish, *Convent of Pleasure*, pp. 220, 223.

65   Ibid., p. 219.

66   Brian, *The V Club*, p. 75.

67   Chaucer, 'The Knight's Tale', p. 56, ll. 2304–10.

68   Chaucer, 'The Monk's Tale', p. 245, ll. 2255–70.

69   Westphal, 'Camilla', p. 232.

70   *The Travels of Sir John Mandeville*, p. 116.

71   Christine de Pizan, *The Book of the City of Ladies*, pp. 4, 42.

72   Ellison, 'Epicoene', ll. 1–7, 9–14.

73   Marvell, 'Upon Appleton House', ll. 94, 106, 120, 205, 257. Appleton House had been a Cistercian nunnery; after it was dissolved the land went to the Fairfax family.

74   For more on literary treatments of Joan's life from the fifteenth to the twentieth century, see Raknem, *Joan of Arc*.

75   Warner observes that '*pucelle*' means 'virgin, but in a special way, with distinct shades connoting youth, innocence, and, paradoxically, nubility' (*Joan of Arc*, p. 22).

76   See McInerney, *Eloquent Virgins*.

77   See Sullivan, *Interrogation of Joan of Arc*, pp. 42–5.

78   Shakespeare, *Henry VI, Part I*, V.iii. 18–19; 22–3.

79   Ibid., V. iv. 36–41, 48–53.

80   Ibid., V. iv. 65, 84, I. vi. 107.

81   Chaucer, 'The Wife of Bath's Prologue', p. 107, ll. 149–50.

82   D'Urfey, 'An Epithalamium', stanza 3. The imagery in epithalamia, while ostensibly celebratory, can also hint at the dangers attending the loss of the virginal state. In her 'Epithalamium', Mrs Anna Letitia Barbauld begins with the familiar comparison of the virgin bride with the dawning day. In the third stanza, however, the maiden is warned that she must not tarry too long, or the flowers that are strewn on her path to the altar 'will begin . . . to fade'. Stanza four sees the 'happy bride' turning red and

white with dread at what is to come, and the final stanza celebrates the triumph of a bellicose Love who demands that she 'be the sacrifice'.

83   Marton, *The Disobedient Virgin*, p. 148.

84   Monroe, *The Greek's Innocent Virgin*, pp. 82–3.

85   Harwood, *Six Reasons to Stay a Virgin*, pp. 90–91.

86   Brian, *The V Club*, p. 98.

87   Barker, 'A Virgin Life', ll. 5–8.

88   Cokain, 'Of Galla', ll. 1–2.

89   'Ephelia', 'Maidenhead', ll. 21, 24.

90   Cunningham, 'A Man to My Mind', ll. 1–2.

91   Cowley, 'Maidenhead', ll. 1, 8, 23–4.

92   Dibdin, 'Ballad', ll. 1–2.

93   Baxter, 'The Hymen', ll. 11–14, 2–4.

94   Broughton, 'Don Giovanni', ll. 8, 11, 13, 1–2.

95   Burton, *Anatomy of Melancholy*, Part III, pp. 418, 244.

96   Ibid., p. 133.

97   Edward, Lord Herbert of Cherbury, 'Green-Sickness Beauty', p. 48, ll. 32–33. See also McFarland, 'The Rhetoric of Medicine', pp. 252–3.

98   Anon., *The Virgins Complaint*, pp. 1–2, 6.

99   Ibid., p. 3.

100   Shakespeare, *A Midsummer Night's Dream*, I. i. 70–74, 75, 77.

101   Cambridge, 'The Virgin Martyr', ll. 6–10.

102   Dickens, *Great Expectations*, p. 87.

103   Newman, 'Re-Membering', p. 47.

104   Many 'coming-of-age' films focus on the loss of virginity as marking entry into adulthood (either physically, spiritually or both). For some examples, see the films listed in the bibliography.

105   Eugenides, *Virgin Suicides*, pp. 146–7, 8, 190–91.

106   Ibid., pp. 169, 186, 188.

107   Ibid., p. 244.

108   Ibid., p. 22.

Chapter 4: 'Repugnant to the Common Good'

1   Knox, *The First Blast*, p. 28.

2   Beck, *Elements*, I, p. 72.

3   Cited in Kennedy, *Eve Was Framed*, p. 111.

4   The body-politic model was used beyond the Middle Ages; see, for

Notes

instance, the opening scene in Shakespeare's *Coriolanus*.

5   Anon., 'The Descryvyng of Mannes Membres', p. 69, ll. 144–7.

6   Camille, 'The Image and the Self', p. 69. See also Nederman and Forhan, eds., *Medieval Political Theory*.

7   *Hoccleve's Works*, pp. 131–2, ll. 3627–9, 3655–7; p. 134, l. 3731.

8   Saunders, *Rape*, p. 75.

9   Wogan-Browne, for instance, points out how the medieval English historiographer William of Malmesbury wrote 'a recuperative English history based on the claim that nowhere else has so many incorrupt saints' bodies' ('Virginity Now and Then', p. 238). See also Ruth Evans, 'Virginities', p. 35. On Edward's virginity, see Huntington, 'Edward the Celibate'.

10 See Bernau, '"Saint, Witch, Man, Maid or Whore?"', p. 215.

11 Camden, *Annales*, Bk. I, pp. 26, 22, 27–8.

12 Jankowski elaborates on this idea: '[Elizabeth's] "marriage" was to be mystical/metaphorical. She was "married" to England in the same way that the Virgin Mary was "married" to God, the father of her child' (*Pure Resistance*, p. 13). For a different view see Hackett, *Virgin Mother*.

13 Yates, *Astraea*, pp. 86–7; cited in King, 'Queen Elizabeth I', 30–31.

14 See Kelly and Leslie, *Menacing Virgins*, p. 18.

15 Chrisafies, writing for the *Guardian* (21 September 2006), notes that 'Mr Le Pen's favoured historical figure has been Joan of Arc, a symbol of the French defeat of foreign invaders. He has statues of her in his house and leads a May Day rally in her honour each year' ('Le Pen Launches Election Battle').

16 On the association of land with woman, see for instance Kolodny, *The Lay of the Land*; Mosse, *Nationalism and Sexuality*, esp. pp. 90–113. For women and national origins, see Geary, *Women*.

17 Ralegh, *Discoverie*, p. 96 and prefatory 'To the Reader'.

18 See King, *Disease of Virgins*, p. 80, and Montrose, 'The Work of Gender', pp. 184–5.

19 Luke Gernon, *A Discourse of Ireland* (*c.* 1620), BL Stowe Mss vol. 28, 5; cited in King, *Disease of Virgins*, p. 81.

20 Klairmont-Lingo, 'The Fate', 341.

21 'Defloration', in *Chambers Paperback Thesaurus* (Edinburgh: Chambers Harrap Publishers Ltd, 1992).

22 Ingebretsen, 'Wigglesworth', p. 22.

23 Douglas, *Purity and Danger*, p.156.

24 Dod and Clever, *A Godly Forme*, sig. A4 and 'The Epistle Dedicatorie'.

25 Vives, *A Very Fruitful and Pleasant Book*, Ch. VII: 'Of the Kepyng of Virginite and Chastitie', sig. G2r-G4v. Miller outlines the book's great popularity: '[T]he book was widely published throughout Europe in thirty-six English, Castilian, French, German, and Italian translations . . . Indeed, the book attempts to formulate a general and broadly applicable regimen for rearing and educating women' ('Metaphor and Mystification', p. 133).

26 It is therefore unsurprising that what Margaret Ferguson calls the 'spectre of an active virginity' lurks threateningly in the psyche of cultures that place such a high value on female purity. The threat of the 'active virgin' is that, in rejecting or escaping the patriarchal control at home, she threatens the 'analogous sphere' of the state as well ('Foreword', pp. 8–9).

27 Kelly and Leslie, *Menacing Virgins*, p. 18.

28 See Peek, 'King by Day', esp. pp. 72–5.

29 See Kelly and Leslie, *Menacing Virgins*, p. 17. Mary Fissell points out that in Early Modern England '[a] common slang term for women's genitals was the word "commodity"' ('Gender and Generation', 438).

30 See Riddy, 'Temporary Virginity', p. 197. Jankowski suggests that, in Early Modern England, 'the necessity for the capitalist to be sure that *all* his children were fathered by him added economic impetus for female marital fidelity and led to the fetishization of chastity' (*Pure Resistance*, p. 80). Weeks makes a similar point in relation to the nineteenth century (*Sex, Politics*, pp. 29–30).

31 'Philogamus', p. 78.

32 Phillips, 'Four Virgins' Tales', p. 89. She concludes that '[p]ower, money and the female body form a nexus of interlocking concerns in social groups including . . . the lower nobility, well-off and less prosperous peasantry and landholding towndwellers' (p. 81).

33 See Karras, *From Boys to Men*, esp. pp. 79–80.

34 Weeks, *Sex, Politics*, p. 30.

35 Fessenden, 'The Other Woman's Sphere', p. 170.

36 Leites, *Puritan Conscience*, p. 16.

37 Wilkes, 'A Letter', p. 30.

38 See Cott, 'Passionlessness'; Haller and Haller, *The Physician*; and Leites, *Puritan Conscience*.

39 See Crawford, 'Sexual Knowledge'.

40 *The Awful Disclosures of Maria Monk* (Bexhill-on-Sea: AKS Books Ltd, 2004).

41 Lees, *Ruling Passions*, p. 73.

Notes

42 'Philogamus', p. 80.

43 Haller and Haller, *The Physician*, pp. 57–8. Here they also point out the parallels between the ways in which medical opinion was mobilized against both feminism and the Civil Rights Movements. In their inferiority to (white) men, (white) women were likened to 'inferior' races.

44 Numerous scholars have shown that the idea of the morally superior woman was used by women to promote their role in the family and society, but it was one thing to do so as a mother and/or wife, another to do so as an umarried woman.

45 On a fascinating account of one contentious alternative for women, see Mumm, *Stolen Daughters*.

46 Clarke, *Sex in Education*, p. 131.

47 See Haller and Haller, *The Physician*, p. 66.

48 Ibid., pp. 67, 84.

49 See Dixon, *Perilous Chastity*, p. 38.

50 See, for instance, Ashley, 'Medieval Courtesy Literature', p. 36.

51 *A Parisian Journal, 1405–99*, pp. 263–4.

52 Richards, *Sex*, p. 25.

53 See Weeks, *Sex, Politics*, p. 160.

54 Cited in Hall, 'Hauling Down', 44.

55 Shalit, *A Return to Modesty*, pp. 43, 47, 149, 157. Such polemics tend to exhibit a lack of familiarity with feminist thought, resulting in reductive and even near-parodic representations of its alleged aims, ignoring the fact that feminism has always been home to a wide range of views. One such crude assertion claims, for instance, that feminism tells women: 'The purpose of female sexuality is to assert power over hapless men, for control, revenge, self-centred pleasure, or forcing a commitment' (Hinlicky, 'Subversive Virginity'). My point is not so much that these writers should agree with all or some feminist thought, but that their critique of it should at least be an informed one.

56 Keller, *The Cult of the Born-Again Virgin*, pp. 3–4.

57 One can also see some similarities in such contemporary writings promoting virginity and abstinence with some feminist thought, particulary in the nineteenth century, though also in the more radical, separatist forms of feminism, which argue that women who engage in heterosexual relations are 'genitally enslaved'. See, for instance, Cline, *Celibacy and Passion*, p. 195.

58 Keller, *The Cult of the Born-Again Virgin*, pp. 3, 28.

59 The view that we live in times that are 'less inhibited and more dangerous'

is also found in more scholarly work; see for instance Brumberg, *The Body Project*, p. 142.

60 Saunders, *Rape*, pp. 3, 21.

61 Ibid., p. 20.

62 Phillips, 'Four Virgins' Tales', p. 85.

63 Saunders, *Rape*, pp. 4, 52. Phillips names some of the main legal treatises of twelfth- and thirteenth-century England: *Glanvill* (c. 1187–9); *Fleta* (late 13th century); *Britton* (c. 1291–2); Bracton's treatise (c. 1218–29) ('Four Virgins' Tales', p. 85). Saunders also refers to Westminster I (1275) and Westminster II (1285) (pp. 59–60). These sources are still referred to by legal texts written several hundred years later.

64 See Phillips, 'Four Virgins' Tales'.

65 See Phillips, 'Written on the Body', pp. 137–8; Saunders, *Rape*, p. 52.

66 *Bracton de legibus*, II, 'De placitis coronae', pp. 414–15; cited in Saunders, *Rape*, pp. 53–4. Phillips argues that secular writings such as *Glanvill* and other 13th-century texts saw rape as a sexual violation and 'felony whether the woman be a virgin or not' ('Four Virgins' Tales', p. 84).

67 Saunders, *Rape*, pp. 85–6.

68 See Phillips, 'Written on the Body', pp. 125–44.

69 Saunders, *Rape*, p. 99.

70 Cooper, *Tracts*, Ch. IV, pp. 24–5; my emphasis. He also adds that 'It may be necessary to enquire how far her lust was excited, or if she experienced any enjoyment. For without an excitation of lust, or the enjoyment of pleasure in the venereal act, no conception can probably take place' (p. 25).

71 Kennedy, *Eve Was Framed*, p. 111. She adds that '[s]imilar words were used by Judge Dean at the Old Bailey in 1990, and countless other judges must be breathing sighs of relief at having escaped press attention'.

72 Phillips, 'Four Virgins' Tales', p. 86.

73 Barbara J. Baines, 'Effacing Rape', 72; see also Bashar, 'Rape in England'. Walker shows that 17th-century legal definitions of rape 'required penile penetration of the vagina' and had to occur without the woman's consent if she was over the age of ten. Under the age of ten she was too young to consent, so it was rape whether or not she consented to it ('Rereading Rape', 3).

74 Walker, 'Rereading Rape', 5.

75 Hale (1609–1676), *Historia placitorum coronae*, I, p. 631. A 1991 edition of the *Encyclopedia Britannica* states that Hale remains 'one of the principal authorities on the common law of criminal offenses' (V, p. 631); in 1992, Kennedy wrote that Hale is 'held responsible for much of the

jurisprudence about rape'. His view that marital rape was an impossibility was not revised in British law until 1991 (*Eve Was Framed*, p. 130).

76   Russell, *A Treatise*, I, p. 802. Russell's *Treatise* was first published in 1819, went through twelve editions and was last published in 1964 (*Dictionary of National Biography*).

77   Beck, *Elements*, I, p. 79. In a footnote to the text he admits that 'there does not exist any true and certain sign of virginity'.

78   Tidy, *Legal Medicine*, II, p. 210.

79   Ibid., p. 210 (latter emphasis mine).

80   Ewell, *A Manual*, Ch. XII. It is not explained why such cases will 'seldom come before the medical jurist'.

81   Ellison, *Lectures*, p. 45.

82   Hale, *Historia placitorum coronae*, I, p. 634.

83   Amos Dean, *Principles of Medical Jurisprudence: Designed for the Professions of Law and Medicine* (New York: Banks & Bros., 1866, *c.* 1850), p. 25.

84   William George Aitchison Robertson, *Manuals of Medical Jurisprudence and Toxicology*, 4th edn (1908; London, 1921), p. 257.

85   Hale, *Historia placitorum coronae*, I, p. 633.

86   Lees, *Ruling Passions*, pp. 73, 3, 17.

87   As the Rape Crisis website explains on its page dedicated to rape myths, 'Research shows that in the majority of cases the rapist is known to the woman. He may be a friend, a workmate, relative or husband. About 50% of rapes occur in the home of the woman or the attacker.'

88   For a brief overview of English and American rape laws, see Herman, 'Rape (Law)'.

89   Hinsliff, 'Law Failing'.

90   Sawyer, '50,000 Rapes'. The same article states that the rate of convictions fell from 24 per cent in 1985.

91   'Rape Convictions Hit Record Low', BBC News, 25 February 2005. Sawyer's article states that research suggests 'only 3 per cent of rape allegations are false' ('50,000 Rapes').

92   Kennedy, *Eve Was Framed*, p. 139.

Chapter 5: The Future of Virginity

1   Weeks, *Sex, Politics*, p. 38.

2   Hall notes, for instance, that '[m]en from the rougher strata of the lower

classes who joined the army and navy, in particular, were regarded as having uncontrolled and probably uncontrollable sexual urges' ('Hauling Down', 39).

3   This is a vast and complex field of study, which I cannot hope to do justice to here; there are many excellent studies on these issues.

4   Carpenter, 'Ambiguity', 127.

5   Naaman, 'Is There Honor in Death?', presented as part of the website for the Atlanta Center for Laparoscopic Urogynecology.

6   Ingrassia, 'Virgin Cool', p. 60.

7   Jemmott and Fry, 'Abstinence Strategy', p. 116.

8   Mebane, Yam, Rimer, 'Sex Education', 583. In her article 'No Sex', Walters cites the following statistics: 'The US National Survey of Family Growth just reported the latest figures, from 2002, showing that 30 per cent of American girls aged 15 to 17 have had sex compared with 38 per cent in 1995 and 31 per cent of boys, compared with 43 per cent in 1995. Teenage pregnancy rates show the US birth rate for 15- to 19-year-olds fell from 62 per 1,000 in 1991 to 43 per 1,000 in 2002 . . . In 2002, the equivalent rate in France was 10 per 1,000 females, in Canada 25 and in Britain, which has the highest rate in western Europe but also has comprehensive sex education, it was 28' (p. 22).

9   'What is the Medical Institute', at <http://www.medinstitute.org>.

10   'Sex is for Loving', in SOON Online Magazine: <http://www.soon.org. uk/problems/sexlove.htm>.

11   Abstinence proponents also address those who have already had sex, as I outlined previously.

12   Ciardullo, 'Advocates'.

13   A recent article in the *Observer* reported that a 'MORI poll of 1,790 adults reveals that people are delaying the moment when they decide to first have sex' in Britain. At the same time a clear majority – '84 per cent' – 'back the recent call from the government's advisers that all schools should teach pupils about sexual behaviour and relationships, not just the basic biology of reproduction, which is the only statutory sex education' (Campbell, 'No Sex Please'). The MORI poll also revealed that 45 per cent of British men and 49 per cent of British women think children are given too little information about sex (23 per cent and 21 per cent respectively thought the amount of information was 'about right', while 13 per cent and 11 per cent respectively thought it was 'too much') ('Sex UK: The Facts', p. 17; see also <www.mori.com>).

Notes

14 Campbell, 'What Teens Really Think about Sex', *Observer*, 21 May 2006, p. 14. For a passionate and insightful review of a TV programme aired on BBC2 entitled *No Sex Please, We're Teenagers*, see Rayner, 'Kiss Chaste', p. 20.

15 See, for instance, Irvine, *Talk about Sex*.

16 See Smith, *Christian America?*

17 Kempner, 'Controversial'.

18 Ciardullo, 'Advocates'.

19 Cited in Levine, 'No-Sex', p. 439. Weeks looks at the wider context when he argues that the 'juncture in the United States in 1979 of New Right political forces and Jerry Falwell's evangelical Moral Majority movement provided a strong cadre of footsoldiers in many parts of the country to ensure Ronald Reagan's Presidential election victories in 1980 and 1984'. In fact, he believes that the 'American New Right had a political agenda – on the economy, race, law and order, defence, and the family – whose origins go well back into the 1960s and before'. Although the connection between conservative politics and evangelical religion is, according to Weeks, less prominent in Britain, he states that they do exist (*Sexuality*, p. 34).

20 Levine, 'No-Sex', p. 439.

21 Mayo, 'Gagged', citing Ingrassia, 'Virgin Cool', p. 60.

22 'Public Support'. The 2004 SIECUS Fact Sheet states that 'Only 30% of American adults agree with the statement "the federal government should fund sex education programs that have 'abstaining from sexual activity' as their only purpose"' ('Public Support'). However, many parents seem to see abstinence as a desirable part of such an education; see Levine, 'No-Sex', p. 440.

23 See Connolly, 'Some Abstinence Programs'.

24 Walters summarizes: 'The federal government will put around $170 million into abstinence-only sex education programmes in schools in 2005, a $30m increase over last year. Bush was pushing for the total to go up to $270m – similar to the money spent on the nation's family planning services, which are experiencing cuts as conservative forces crack down on contraception and abortion.' Another worrying aspect Walters highlights concerns the *quality* of abstinence-only curricula, claiming that some of the more 'radical' abstinence-only curricula contained misinformation or misrepresented medical evidence ('No Sex', p. 22).

25 Levine, 'No-Sex', p. 439.

26   Kempner, 'Controversial'.

27   Levine, 'No-Sex', pp. 439–40. See also Landry, Kaeser, and Richards, 'Abstinence Promotion'.

28   Mebane, Yam, Rimer, 'Sex Education', 584. For similar oppositions in the UK, see Lees, *Ruling Passions*, p. 39; and Arnot and Barton, eds., *Voicing Concerns*.

29   See <www.soon.org.uk/problems/sexlove.htm>. The 'ideal' relationship that is being promised here is arguably just as elusive as the ideal family life that is portrayed as easily achievable in these debates.

30   Levine, 'No-Sex', p. 453, n. 2. See also Levine, *Harmful to Minors*.

31   Kantor, 'Scared Chaste?'. Kantor points out that 'fear-based programs' are to be distinguished from some 'abstinence-based' curricula that 'provide support for postponing sexual behavior without utilizing scare tactics to achieve that end'.

32   See Ciardullo, 'Advocates'.

33   Kempner, 'Controversial'.

34   Mayo, 'Gagged'.

35   Mayo, 'Gagged'. In an article for the *Guardian*, Armstrong (author of *The Battle for God: A History of Fundamentalism*) states that 'The US infant mortality rate is only the 42nd best in the world; the average baby has a better chance of surviving in Havana or Beijing; infant mortality rates are unacceptably high among those who cannot afford adequate healthcare, especially in the African-American community' ('Comment and Debate', p. 24). It should be noted once more that it would be misleading to use the umbrella term 'evangelicals' (Armstrong uses 'fundamentalists' instead) as though this denoted a single, well-defined group. Wallis, a prominent evangelical, for instance decries what he calls 'fundamentalist religion', which he sees as influencing the political agenda and discourse of the current administration (*God's Politics*, p. 35).

36   See also Leites, *Puritan Conscience*, esp. p. 10.

37   See ibid., p. 152.

38   Pivar, *Purity Crusade*, pp. 259, 152.

39   Levine, 'No-Sex', p. 449. Weeks locates the heightened parental involvement in – and control of – adolescent sexuality in the nineteenth century (*Sex, Politics*, pp. 50–51).

40   Virginity pledges are promoted by religious – mostly evangelical – groups, and are frequently linked to support for abstinence-only education. The largest promoters of such pledges are True Love Waits and Silver Ring

Thing. On their impact in the UK, see Hinsliff, 'Banned', p. 3. Catholic groups in Britain have also run 'chastity workshops'; see Fowler, 'Just Say No', p. 58.

41 Mebane, Yam and Rimer, 'Sex Education', pp. 588–9.

42 'Virginity Pledges Do Not Predict Risk', 19. For a more detailed study whose findings suggest that religiosity *is* an important factor in delaying sexual intercourse, while virginity pledges are not, see Rostosky, Regnerus and Wright, 'Coital Debut'.

43 Mebane, Yam and Rimer, 'Sex Education', pp. 603, 585.

44 Brocato, 'U.S.-Based Opposition'. In 2003 the US House of Representatives stipulated that of the $15 billion that were to be spent to combat AIDS worldwide, $5 billion *had* to be used to promote abstinence-education programmes (see Bernau, 'Girls on Film', p. 97).

45 Brocato, 'U.S.-Based Opposition'. See also Kaplan on the dramatic increase in HIV infections (almost doubling from '70,000 in 2003 to 130,000 in 2005') in Uganda, whose 'ambitious HIV prevention campaign, which involved massive condom distribution, explicit information about transmission, and messages about delaying sex and reducing numbers of partners', begun in 1986, was replaced, starting in 2002, with an abstinence-only message, supported by US-based evangelical organizations ('Fairy-Tale Failure', 7).

46 Carpenter, 'Ambiguity'.

47 Carpenter states: '[D]espite this apparent consensus, the definition of virginity remains somewhat ambiguous. In the one study (to my knowledge) to investigate explicitly how young people define virginity loss, only four fifths of respondents agreed that a woman would lose her virginity "if her vagina [was] fully penetrated by a penis". Furthermore, anecdotal evidence suggests that young lesbians and gay men have recently begun to reframe virginity loss as including sex between same-sex partners, rather than deeming virginity loss as irrelevant to their own experiences as was common in the past' ('Ambiguity').

48 In fact, the responses to the question of whether a woman who was raped was no longer a virgin drew the most divergent responses: 'Nearly two thirds of women in the study said that rape could never or only technically constitute virginity loss, compared with only half of men' (Carpenter, 'Ambiguity').

49 It is also important to consider the different attitudes to virginity that exist in different communities in the US; 80 per cent of Carpenter's interviewees

were white. For different attitudes to virginity and its loss, see, for instance, Jemmott and Fry, 'Abstinence'; Okazaki, 'Influences of Culture'; and Villaruel, 'Cultural Influences'.

50 Sommers and Sommers, *Everything You Need to Know About Virginity*. Luadzers' approach to 'Pure Virgin Sex' in *Virgin Sex* is a somewhat awkward amalgamation of the two positions.

Bibliography

Abbreviations

EEBO   Early English Books Online
            <http://eebo.chadwyck.com/home>
LION   Literature Online
            <http://lion.chadwyck.co.uk/>
ECCO   Eighteenth Century Collections Online
            <http://www.gale.com/EighteenthCentury/>
SIECUS   Sexuality Information and Education Council of the US, Inc.,
            Report
            <http://www.siecus.org/>
ScienceDirect <http://www.sciencedirect.com/>
MML   The Making of Modern Law: Legal Treatises 1800–1926
            <http://www.galeuk.com/trials/moml>

Films

All the Real Girls. Dir. David Gordon Green. 2003. Sony Picture Classics.
American Virgin. Dir. Jean-Pierre Marois. 2000. Studio Home Entertainment.
Chasing Amy. Dir. Kevin Smith. 1997. Miramax Films.
Grease. Dir. Randal Kleiser. 1977. Paramount Pictures.
Kids. Dir. Larry Clark. 1995. Shining Excalibur Pictures.
Live Virgin. Dir. Jean-Pierre Marois. 1999. Vertigo Productions.
Stealing Beauty. Dir. Bernardo Bertolucci. 1996. Fox Searchlight Pictures.

Virgins

The Forty-Year-Old Virgin. Dir. Judd Apatow. 2005. Universal Pictures.
The Last American Virgin. Dir. Boaz Davidson. 1982. The Cannon Group, Inc.
The Sound of Music. Dir. Robert Wise. 1965. Twentieth-Century Fox.
The Virgin Suicides. Dir. Sofia Coppola. 2000. American Zoetrope.

Websites

Atlanta Center for Laparoscopic Urogynecology:
   <http://www.urogynecologychannel.net/> (accessed 1 February 2007)
Guardian Unlimited: <www.guardian.co.uk>
Ipsos Mori: <http://www.mori.com> (accessed 1 February 2007)
Pamela Loftus, MD: <http://medpages.obgyn.net/docdetail.cfm?sn=23751>
   (accessed 1 February 2007)
Pamela Loftus, MD: <http://www.labiaplasty.org> (accessed 1 February 2007)
Liberty Women's Health Care: <http://www.libertywomenshealth.com/9html>
   (accessed 21 January 2005)
Rape Crisis England and Wales: <http://www.rapecrisis.org.uk> (accessed 1
   February 2007)
'Secondary/ "Renewed" Virginity', at <http://www.geocities.com/thevirginclub/
   Secondary.htm?200611> (accessed 1 February 2007)
'Sex is for Loving', SOON Online Magazine: <http://www.soon.org.uk /problems/
   sexlove.htm> (accessed 1 February 2007)
'The Hymen': <http://www.rotten.com/library/sex/hymen/> (accessed 1 February
   2007)
The Labiaplasty Master Surgery Center of New York: <http://www.labiadoctor.
   com/> (accessed 1 February 2007)
The Laser Vaginal Rejuvenation Institute of Los Angeles: <http://www.drmatlock.
   com/media.htm> (accessed 1 February 2007)
The Medical Institute: <http://www.medinstitute.org> (accessed 1 February 2007)

Books and Articles

A Parisian Journal, 1405–99, trans. Janet Shirley (Oxford: Oxford University
   Press, 1968).
Aelred of Rievaulx, 'The Nun of Watton', trans. in John Boswell, *The Kindness
   of Strangers: The Abandonment of Children in Western Europe from Late
   Antiquity to the Renaissance* (1988; Chicago: The University of Chicago
   Press, 1998), pp. 452–8.

Bibliography

Anon., 'The Country Miss New Come in Fashion; or, A Farewel to the Pockifi'd Town Miss' (London, 1677), EEBO.

— 'The Descryvyng of Mannes Membres', in *Twenty-Six Political and Other Poems from the Oxford MSS. Digby 102 and Douce 322*, ed. J. Kail, Early English Text Society, 124 (London, 1904), pp. 64–9.

— 'The Loving Chamber-Maid; or, Vindication of a Departed Maidenhead' (West Smithfield, 1675), EEBO.

— *A Looking-Glasse for the Ranters* (London, 1653), pp. 16–17, EEBO.

— *Ancrene Wisse*, in *Anchoritic Spirituality: 'Ancrene Wisse' and Associated Works*, trans. Anne Savage and Nicholas Watson (New York: Paulist Press, 1991), pp. 41–207.

— *Holy Maidenhood*, in *Anchoritic Spirituality: 'Ancrene Wisse' and Associated Works*, trans. Anne Savage and Nicholas Watson (New York: Paulist Press, 1991), pp. 223–43.

— *The Virgins Complaint for the Losse of Their Sweet-hearts* (1646), EEBO.

Aristotle's Compleat and Experience'd Midwife in Two Parts (London, 1700), EEBO.

Armstrong, Karen, 'Comment and Debate: Bush's Fondness for Fundamentalism is Courting Disaster at Home and Abroad', *Guardian*, 31 July 2006, p. 24.

Arnot, M., and L. Barton, *Voicing Concerns: Sociological Perspectives on Contemporary Education Reforms* (London: Triangle, 1992).

Ashley, Kathleen M., 'Medieval Courtesy Literature and Dramatic Mirrors of Female Conduct', in *The Ideology of Conduct: Essays on Literature and the History of Sexuality*, ed. Nancy Armstrong and Leonard Tennenhouse (New York and London: Methuen, 1987), pp. 25–38.

Astruc, Jean, *A Treatise on the Diseases of Women*, 2 vols (London, 1762), EEBO.

Avery, Giles B., *Sketches of Shakers and Shakerism: Synopsis of Theology of United Society of Believers in Christ's Second Appearing* (Albany, NY: Weed, Parsons and Company, 1884).

Ayres, Philip, 'Emb. 9. Love a ticklish Game', from *Emblems of Love* (1683), LION.

Baines, Barbara J., 'Effacing Rape in Early Modern Representation', *English Literary History*, 65.1 (1998), 69–98.

Barbauld, Mrs Anna Letitia, 'Epithalamium', from *The Works* (1825), LION.

Barker, Jane, 'A Virgin Life', from *Poetical Recreations* (1688), LION.

Bashar, Nazife, 'Rape in England between 1550 and 1700', in *The Sexual Dynamics of History: Men's Power, Women's Resistance* (London: Pluto Press, 1983).

Virgins

Baxter, James K., 'The Hymen', from *Collected Poems* (1980), LION.

Beale, John S., 'Labour, with the Hymen Unbroken', *Lancet*, 74.1873 (23 July 1859), pp. 98–9, ScienceDirect.

Beck, Theodric Romeyn, *Elements of Medical Jurisprudence*, 2 vols. (Albany, NY, 1823), MML.

Benson, Larry D., gen. ed., *The Riverside Chaucer* (Oxford: Oxford University Press, 1988).

Bentley, Thomas, *The Fift Lampe of Virginitie* (London: H. Denham, 1582), EEBO.

Bernau, Anke, '"Saint, Witch, Man, Maid or Whore?" Joan of Arc and Writing History', in *Medieval Virginities*, ed. Anke Bernau, Ruth Evans and Sarah Salih (Cardiff: University of Wales Press, 2003), pp. 214–33.

— 'Gender and Sexuality', in *A Companion to Middle English Hagiography*, ed. Sarah Salih (Cambridge: Boydell and Brewer, 2006), pp. 104–21.

— 'Girls on Film: Medieval Virginity in the Cinema', in *The Medieval Hero on Screen: Representations from Beowulf to Buffy*, ed. Martha Driver and Sid Ray (London: McFarland, 2004), pp. 94–114.

Bertrams, Wilhelm, SJ, *The Celibacy of the Priest: Meaning and Basis*, trans. Rev. P. Byrne, SM (German original, 1960; Westminster: St Paul Publications, 1963).

Bloch, Howard R., *Medieval Misogyny and the Invention of Western Romantic Love* (Chicago: University of Chicago Press, 1991).

Blume, Judy, *Forever* (1975; London: Macmillan Children's Books, 2001).

Boucé, Paul-Gabriel, 'Some Sexual Beliefs and Myths in Eighteenth-Century Britain', in *Sexuality in Eighteenth-Century Britain*, ed. Paul-Gabriel Boucé (Manchester: Manchester University Press, 1982), pp. 28–46.

Bracton de legibus et consuetudinibus Angliae: Bracton on the Laws and Customs of England, ed. George E. Woodbine, trans. Samuel E. Thorne, 4 vols. (Cambridge, Mass.: Belknap Press of Harvard University Press, in assoc. with Selden Society, 1968–77).

Brian, Kate, *The V Club* (London: Simon and Schuster, 2004).

Brocato, Vanessa, 'U.S.-Based Opposition to Sexual and Reproductive Rights Goes International', *SIECUS Report*, 32.4 (Fall 2004), p. 22 (6).

Broughton, James, 'Don Giovanni to the Very Nice New Virgin', from *Packing Up For Paradise: Selected Poems 1946–1996* (1997), LION.

Broumas, Olga, and T. Begley, 'I Don't Know Virgin', from *Sappho's Gymnasium* (1994), LION.

Brumberg, Joan Jacobs, *The Body Project: An Intimate History of American Girls* (New York: Vintage Books, 1998).

Bibliography

Brundage, James A., *Law, Sex, and Christian Society in Medieval Europe* (Chicago: University of Chicago Press, 1987).

Burton, Robert, *The Anatomy of Melancholy*, intro. William H. Gass (New York: New York Review Books, 2001).

Cadden, Joan, 'Western Medicine and Natural Philosophy' in *Handbook of Medieval Sexuality*, ed. Vern L. Bullough and James A. Brundage (New York: Garland Publishing, 1996), pp. 51–80.

— *Meanings of Sex Difference in the Middle Ages: Medicine, Science, and Culture* (Cambridge: Cambridge University Press, 1993).

Cambridge, Ada, 'The Virgin Martyr', from *The Hand in the Dark and Other Poems* (1913), LION.

Camden, William, *Annales: The True and Royall History of the Famous Empresse Elizabeth, Queene of England, France, and Ireland, etc.* (orig. publ. 1586; 1625), EEBO.

Camille, Michael, 'The Image and the Self: Unwriting Late Medieval Bodies', in *Framing Medieval Bodies*, ed. Sarah Kay and Miri Rubin (Manchester: Manchester University Press, 1994), pp. 62–99.

Campbell, Denis, 'No Sex Please Until We're At Least 17 Years Old, We're British', *Observer*, 22 January 2006, <http://observer.guardian.co.uk/uk_news story/0,,1692307,00.html>.

— 'What Teens Really Think about Sex', *Observer*, 21 May 2006, p. 14.

Carpenter, Laura M., 'Gender and the Meaning and Experience of Virginity Loss in the Contemporary United States', *Gender and Society*, 16.3 (June 2002), 345–65.

— 'The Ambiguity of "Having Sex": The Subjective Experience of Virginity Loss in the United States (Statistical Data Included)', *Journal of Sex Research*, 38.2 (May 2001), p. 127.

Cavendish, Margaret (Duchess of Newcastle), *The Convent of Pleasure and Other Plays*, ed. Anne Shaver (Baltimore and London: Johns Hopkins University Press, 1999).

Chaucer, Geoffrey, 'The Knight's Tale', in *The Riverside Chaucer*, pp. 37–66.

— 'The Monk's Tale', in *The Riverside Chaucer*, pp. 241–52.

— 'The Physician's Tale', in *The Riverside Chaucer*, pp. 190–93.

— 'The Wife of Bath's Prologue', in *The Riverside Chaucer*, pp. 105–16.

Chrisafies, Angelique, 'Le Pen Launches Election Battle', *Guardian*, 21 September 2006.

Christine de Pizan, *The Book of the City of Ladies*, trans. Earl Jeffrey (New York: Persea Books, 1982).

Ciardullo, Maxwell, 'Advocates on Both Sides Are as Passionate as Ever: SIECUS Controversy Report 2004–05 School Year', *SIECUS Report*, 33.4 (Fall 2005), p. 4 (16).

Clare, John, 'A Maiden-Haid', from *The Early Poems* (1989), LION.

Clark, Elizabeth, and Herbert Richardson, eds., *Women and Religion: A Feminist Sourcebook of Christian Thought* (New York: Harper and Row, 1977).

Clarke, Edward H., *Sex in Education; or, A Fair Chance for Girls* (Boston: J. R. Osgood, 1873).

Cleland, John, *Fanny Hill; or, Memoirs of a Woman of Pleasure* (1748, 1749; London: Penguin Popular Classics, 1994).

Cline, Sally, *Celibacy and Passion* (1993; repr. Optima, 1994).

Cokain, Aston, 'Of Galla', from *Small Poems of Divers Sorts* (1658), LION.

Coley, James Milman, 'On Imperforate Hymen, and Retention of Urine Therefrom', *Lancet*, 20.512 (22 June 1833), 395–6, ScienceDirect.

Connolly, Ceci, 'Some Abstinence Programs Mislead Teens, Report Says', *Washington Post*, 2 December 2004, <http://www.washingtonpost.com/wp_dyn/articles/A26623-2004dec/.html>.

Cooper, Thomas, *Tracts on Medical Jurisprudence* (Philadelphia, 1819), MML.

Cott, Nancy, 'Passionlessness: An Interpretation of Victorian Sexual Ideology, 1790–1850', *Signs: Journal of Women in Culture and Society*, 4.2 (1978), 219–36.

Cowley, Abraham, 'Maidenhead', from *The Works* (1905–6), LION.

Crawford, Patricia, 'Sexual Knowledge in England, 1500–1750', in *Sexual Knowledge, Sexual Science: The History of Attitudes to Sexuality*, ed. Roy Porter and Mikuláš Teich (Cambridge: Cambridge University Press, 1994), pp. 82–106.

Crooke, Helkiah, *Mikrokosmographia* (London, 1615), EEBO.

Culpeper, Nicholas, *The Idea of Practical Physick* (London, 1657), EEBO.

Cunningham, John, 'A Man to My Mind', from *Poems, chiefly Pastoral* (1771), LION.

D'Urfey, Thomas, 'An Epithalamium Sung at the Marriage of Lady W–', from *A New Collection of Songs and Poems* (1683), EEBO.

Dannenfeldt, Karl H., 'Egyptian Mumia: The Sixteenth Century Experience and Debate', *Sixteenth Century Journal*, 16.2 (1985), 163–80.

Davies, Jon, and Gerard Loughlin, eds., *Sex These Days: Essays on Theology, Sexuality and Society* (Sheffield: Sheffield Academic Press, 1997).

Davies, Redfern, 'Syphilis, with the Hymen Unbroken', *Lancet*, 74.1870 (2 July 1859), p. 7, ScienceDirect.

Dean, Amos, *Principles of Medical Jurisprudence: Designed for the Professions of Law and Medicine* (New York: Banks & Bros., 1866, *c.* 1850), MML.

Bibliography

Dibdin, Charles, 'Ballad', from 'Spirits of Distress, of Ev'ry Occupation', in *A Collection of Songs, Selected from the Works of Mr. Dibdin*, 2 vols. (1814), LION.

Dickens, Charles, *Great Expectations*, ed. Angus Calder (1965; London: Penguin Books, 1985).

Dixon, Laurinda S., *Perilous Chastity: Women and Illness in Pre-Enlightenment Art and Medicine* (Ithaca and London: Cornell University Press, 1995).

Dod, John, and Robert Clever, *A Godly Forme of Houshold Gouernment for the Ordering of Priuate Families* (1630), EEBO.

Dolben, Digby Mackworth, 'Pro Castitate', from *The Poems* (1915), LION.

Douglas, Mary, *Purity and Danger: An Analysis of Concept of Pollution and Taboo* (1966; London and New York: Routledge, 2004).

Duganne, A. J. H., 'The Three Maries', from *Poetical Works* (1865), LION.

Edward, Lord Herbert of Cherbury, 'The Green-Sickness Beauty', in *Minor Poets of the Seventeenth Century: Herbert of Cherbury, Thomas Carew, Sir John Suckling*, ed. R. G. Howarth (1931; London: Dent, 1953), pp. 47–8.

Elkins, Sharon, *Holy Women of Twelfth-Century England* (Chapel Hill and London: University of North Carolina Press, 1988).

Elliot, Elisabeth, *Passion and Purity: Learning to Bring Your Love Life under Christ's Control* (1984; Grand Rapids, Mich.: Fleming H. Revell, 2002).

Elliott, Dyan, *Fallen Bodies: Pollution, Sexuality, and Demonology in the Middle Ages* (Philadelphia: University of Pennsylvania Press, 1999).

Ellis, Bret Easton, *Rules of Attraction* (1987; London: Pan Books, 1988).

Ellison, Andrew, *Lectures on Medical Jurisprudence* (Kirksville, Mo.: J.A. Quintal, J. F. Janisch, 1902?, c. 1899), MML.

Ellison, Henry, 'Epicoene, or Strong-Minded Women', from *Stones from the Quarry* (1875), LION.

'Ephelia', 'Maidenhead: Written at the Request of a Friend' (1647), in *Kissing the Rod: An Anthology of Seventeenth-Century Women's Verse*, ed. Germaine Greer, Jeslyn Medoff, Melinda Sansone and Susan Hastings (London: Virago Press, 1988), p. 278.

Eugenides, Jeffrey, *The Virgin Suicides* (1993; London: Bloomsbury, 2002).

Evans, G. Blakemore, et al., eds., *The Riverside Shakespeare* (Boston: Houghton Mifflin Company, 1974).

Evans, Ruth, 'Virginities', in *The Cambridge Companion to Medieval Women's Writing*, ed. Carolyn Dinshaw and David Wallace (Cambridge: Cambridge University Press, 2003), pp. 21–39.

Ewell, Marshall Davis, *A Manual of Medical Jurisprudence for the Use of*

Students at Law and of Medicine (Boston: Little, Brown, 1887), MML.

Ferguson, Margaret W., 'Foreword', in *Menacing Virgins*, ed. Kelly and Leslie, pp. 7–14.

Fessenden, Tracy, 'The Other Woman's Sphere: Nuns, Prostitutes, and the Medicalization of Middle-Class Domesticity', in *The Puritan Origins of American Sex*, ed. Tracy Fessenden, Magdalena J. Zaborowska, and Nicholas Radel (New York and London: Routledge, 2001), pp. 169–90.

Fissell, Mary, 'Gender and Generation: Representing Reproduction in Early Modern England', *Gender and History*, 7.3 (November 1995), 433–56.

Fogel, Catherine Ingram, and Diane Lauver, eds., *Sexual Health Promotion* (Philadelphia, London, Toronto, Montreal, Sydney, Tokyo: W. B. Saunders Company, 1990).

Fordyce, James, 'Sermon IV: On Female Virtue', from *Sermons to Young Women* (1766), in *Women in the Eighteenth Century*, ed. Jones, item 4.13, pp. 176–9.

Foster, Lawrence, *Religion and Sexuality: Three American Communal Experiments of the Nineteenth Century* (New York: Oxford University Press, 1981).

Fowler, Rebecca, 'Just Say No', *Observer Special Magazine: Sex Uncovered*, 27 October 2002, pp. 56–61.

Freud, Sigmund, 'The Taboo of Virginity', in *The Standard Edition of the Complete Psychological Works of Sigmund Freud*, trans. James Strachey, in collaboration with Anna Freud and the assistance of Alix Strachey and Alan Tyson, XI (London: Hogarth Press, 1957), pp. 192–208.

Geary, Patrick J., *Women at the Beginning: Origin Myths from the Amazons to the Virgin Mary* (Princeton: Princeton University Press, 2006).

Greg, Dr, and Michael Smalley, 'A Renewed Virginity', <www.christianwomen-today.com/womenmen/virginity.html> (accessed 1 February 2007).

Guillaume de Lorris and Jean de Meun, *The Romance of the Rose*, trans. and ed. Frances Horgan (Oxford: Oxford University Press, 1994).

Hackett, Helen, *Virgin Mother, Maiden Queen: Elizabeth I and the Cult of the Virgin Mary* (Basingstoke: Macmillan, 1995).

Hale, Sir Matthew, *Historia placitorum coronae*; *The History of the Pleas of the Crown*, 1st American edition, with notes and references . . . by W.A. Stokes and E. Ingersoll, 2 vols. (Philadelphia, 1847), MML.

Hall, Lesley, 'Hauling Down the Double Standard: Feminism, Social Purity and Sexual Science in Late Nineteenth-Century Britain', *Gender and History* 16.1 (April 2004), 36–56.

Haller, John S., Jr, and Robin M. Haller, *The Physician and Sexuality in Victorian America* (Chicago: University of Illinois Press, 1974).

Bibliography

Harris, Joshua, *I Kissed Dating Goodbye* (Sisters, Oregon: Multnomah Publishers, 1997).

Harwood, Louise, *Six Reasons to Stay a Virgin* (London: Pan Books, 2003).

Henry, A. M., 'The Mystery of Virginity', in *Religious Life v Chastity: Being the English Version of 'La Chasteté' in 'Problèmes de la Religieuse d'aujour-d'hui'*, trans. Lancelot C. Sheppard (London: Blackfriars Publications, 1955), pp. 79–115.

Herman, Susan N., 'Rape (Law)' <http://encarta.msn.com/encyclope-dia_761564013/Rape_(law).html> (accessed 1 February 2007).

Herrick, Robert, 'To the Virgins, to Make Much of Time', from *Hesperides* (1648), LION.

Heyrick, Thomas, 'Advice to a Virgin', from *Miscellany Poems* (1691), LION.

Hill, Aaron, 'Advice to the Virgins, to Guard against Flattery', from *The Works* (1753), LION.

Hinlicky, Sarah E., 'Subversive Virginity', *First Things: A Monthly Journal of Religion and Public Life*, 86 (October 1998), p. 14 (3).

Hinsliff, Gaby, 'Banned: Schoolgirls are Forced to Take Off Chastity Rings – Or Be Ordered Out of Lessons', *Observer*, 18 June 2006, p. 3.

— 'Law Failing Rape Victims, Says QC', *Observer*, 31 July 2005, <http://observer.guardian.co.uk/uk_news/story/0,,1539837,00.html>.

Hoccleve's Works: The Regement of Princes, ed. Frederick J. Furnivall, Early English Text Society, extra series, 72 (London: Kegan Paul, Trench, Trübner, 1897).

Holmes, Oliver Wendell, 'To a Blank Sheet of Paper', from *The Complete Poetical Works* (1912), LION.

Huntington, Joanna, 'Edward the Celibate, Edward the Saint: Virginity in the Construction of Edward the Confessor', in *Medieval Virginities*, ed. Bernau, Evans and Salih, pp. 119–39.

Ingebretsen, Ed, 'Wigglesworth, Mather, Starr: Witch-Hunts and General Wickedness in Public', in *The Puritan Origins*, ed. Fessenden, Zabrowska and Radel, pp. 21–40.

Ingram, John K., 'VII. The Interpreters', from *Sonnets* (1900), LION.

Ingrassia, Michelle, 'Virgin Cool', *Newsweek*, 17 October 1994, p. 60.

Innes, Mary M., trans. and intro., *The Metamorphoses of Ovid* (London: Penguin Books, 1955).

Irvine, Janice M., *Talk about Sex: The Battles over Sex Education in the United States* (Berkeley: University of California Press, 2002).

Jacquart, Danielle, and Claude Thomasset, *Sexuality and Medicine in the Middle Ages*, trans. Matthew Adamson (Princeton: Princeton University Press, 1988).

Jankowski, Theodora A., *Pure Resistance: Queer Virginity in Early Modern English Drama* (Philadelphia: University of Pennsylvania Press, 2000).

Jemmott, John B., III, and Dana Fry, 'The Abstinence Strategy for Reducing Sexual Risk Behavior', in *Beyond Condoms: Alternative Approaches to HIV Prevention*, ed. Ann O'Leary (New York: Kluwer Academic Publishers, 2002), pp. 109–45.

Jones, Vivien, ed., *Women in the Eighteenth Century: Constructions of Femininity* (London: Routledge, 1990).

Kantor, Leslie M., '1992 Scared Chaste? Fear-Based Educational Curricula', *SIECUS Report*, 32. (Spring 2004), p. 32 (2).

Kaplan, Esther, 'Fairy-Tale Failure', *The American Prospect*, 17.7 (July/August 2006), p. 9 (1).

Karras, Ruth Mazo, *From Boys to Men: Formations of Masculinity in Late Medieval Europe* (Philadelphia: University of Pennsylvania Press, 2003).

Keller, Wendy, *The Cult of the Born-Again Virgin: How Single Women Can Reclaim Their Sexual Power* (Deerfield Beach, Florida: Health Communications, 1999).

Kelly, Kathleen Coyne, 'Menaced Masculinity and Imperiled Virginity in Malory's *Morte Darthur*, in *Menacing Virgins*, pp. 97–114.

— and Marina Leslie, eds., *Menacing Virgins: Representing Virginity in the Middle Ages and Renaissance* (London: Associated University Presses, 1999).

— *Performing Virginity and Testing Chastity in the Middle Ages*, Routledge Research in Medieval Studies, 2 (London: Routledge, 2000).

Kempner, Martha E., 'A Controversial Decade: Ten Years of Tracking Debates around Sexuality Education', *SIECUS Report*, 32.2 (Spring 2004), p. 33 (1).

Kendall, William, 'X. Female Beauty', from *Poems* (1793), LION.

Kennedy, Helena, *Eve Was Framed: Women and British Justice* (London: Chatto and Windus, 1992).

King, Helen, *The Disease of Virgins: Green Sickness, Chlorosis and the Problems of Puberty* (London and New York: Routledge, 2003).

King, John N., 'Queen Elizabeth I: Representations of the Virgin Queen', *Renaissance Quarterly*, 43.1 (Spring 1990), 30–74.

Klairmont-Lingo, Alison, 'The Fate of Popular Terms for Female Anatomy in the Age of Print', *French Historical Studies*, 22.3 (1999), 335–49.

Knox, John, *The First Blast of the Trumpet Against the Monstrous Regiment of Women* (1558), EEBO.

Kolodny, Annette, *The Lay of the Land: Metaphor as Experience and History in American Life and Letters* (Chapel Hill: University of North Carolina Press, 1975).

Bibliography

Landry, David J., Lisa Kaeser and Cory L. Richards, 'Abstinence Promotion and the Provision of Information about Contraception in Public School District Sexuality Education Policies', *Family Planning Perspectives*, 31.6 (November/December 1999), 280–86.

Lees, Sue, *Ruling Passions: Sexual Violence, Reputation and the Law* (Buckingham: Open University Press, 1997).

Leites, Edmund, *The Puritan Conscience and Modern Sexuality* (New Haven: Yale University Press, 1986).

Lemay, Helen Rodnite, ed. and trans., *Women's Secrets: A Translation of Pseudo-Albertus Magnus' 'De Secretis Mulierum' with Commentaries* (New York: State University of New York Press, 1992).

Levine, Judith, 'No-Sex Education: From "Chastity" to "Abstinence"', in *Sexualities: Identities, Behaviors, and Society*, ed. Michael S. Kimmel and Rebecca F. Plante (Oxford: Oxford University Press, 2004), pp. 438–55.

— *Harmful to Minors: The Perils of Protecting Children from Sex* (London and Minneapolis: University of Minnesota Press, 2002).

Luadzers, Darcy, *Virgin Sex* (Columbia, South Carolina: Palmetto Tree Press, 2004).

Luther, Martin, 'The Estate of Marriage', in *Women and Religion: A Feminist Sourcebook of Christian Thought*, ed. Elizabeth Clark and Herbert Richardson (New York: Harper and Row, 1977), pp. 135–42.

Mandeville, Bernard, *The Virgin Unmask'd: or, Female Dialogue Betwixt an Elderly Maiden Lady, and her Niece, on Several Diverting Discourses on Love, Marriage, Memoirs and Morals of the Times, by Bernard Mandeville* (London, 1709).

Marton, Sandra, *The Disobedient Virgin* (New York: Harlequin, 2005).

Marvell, Andrew, 'To His Coy Mistress', from *Miscellaneous Poems* (1681), LION.

— 'Upon Appleton House, to My Lord Fairfax', from *Miscellaneous Poems* (1681), LION.

Mayo, Chris, 'Gagged and Bound: Sex Education, Secondary Virginity, and the Welfare Reform Act', in *Philosophy of Education* (1998), <http://www.ed.uiuc.edu/eps/PES-Yearbook/1998/mayo.html>.

McFarland, Ronald E., 'The Rhetoric of Medicine: Lord Herbert's and Thomas Carew's Poems of Green-Sickness', *Journal of the History of Medicine* (July 1975), 250–58.

McInerney, Maud Burnett, *Eloquent Virgins from Thecla to Joan of Arc* (Basingstoke: Palgrave, 2003).

Mebane, Felicia E., Eileen A. Yam and Barbara K. Rimer, 'Sex Education and the

News: Lessons From How Journalists Framed Virginity Pledges', *Journal of Health Communication*, 11 (2006), 583–606.

Merritt, Diane, 'Vulvar and Genital Trauma in Pediatric and Adolescent Gynecology', *Adolescent and Pediatric Gynecology*, 16.5 (October 2004), 371–81.

Middleton, Thomas, and William Rowley, *The Changeling*, ed. Joost Daalder, 2nd edn (1990; London: A&C Black, 1994).

Miller, Nancy Weitz, 'Metaphor and Mystification of Chastity in Vives's *Instruction of a Cristen Woman*', in *Menacing Virgins* ed. Kelly and Leslie, pp. 132–45.

Monroe, Lucy, *The Greek's Innocent Virgin* (New York: Harlequin, 2005).

Montrose, Louis Adrian, 'The Work of Gender in the Discourse of Discovery', in *New World Encounters*, ed. Stephen Greenblatt (Berkeley and London: University of California Press) pp. 177–217.

Morey, Ann-Janine, *Religion and Sexuality in American Literature*, Cambridge Studies in American Literature and Culture, 57 (Cambridge: Cambridge University Press, 1992).

Mosse, George L., *Nationalism and Sexuality: Respectability and Abnormal Sexuality in Modern Europe* (New York: Howard Fertig, 1985).

Mumm, Susan, *Stolen Daughters, Virgin Mothers: Anglican Sisterhoods in Victorian Britain* (London and New York: Leicester University Press, 1999).

Munich, Adrienne Auslander, 'What Lily Knew', in *Virginal Sexuality and Textuality in Victorian Literature*, ed. Lloyd Davis (Albany: State University of New York Press, 1993), pp. 143–57.

Naaman, Lara, 'Is There Honor in Death?', <http://www.urogynecologychannel.net/hymen.php> (accessed 1 February 2007).

Nederman, Cary J., and Kate Langdon Forhan, eds., *Medieval Political Theory: A Reader: The Quest for the Body Politic, 1100–1400* (London and New York: Routledge, 1993).

Newman, Kathy, 'Re-Membering an Interrupted Conversation: The Mother/Virgin Split', *TRIVIA*, 2 (1983), 45–63.

Nilsen, Alleen Pace, 'Virginity: A Metaphor We Live By', *Humor: International Journal of Humor Research*, 3.1 (1990), 3–15.

Okazaki, Sumie, 'Influences of Culture on Asian Americans' Sexuality', in *Sexualities: Identities, Behaviors, and Society*, ed. by Michael S. Kimmel and Rebecca F. Plante (Oxford: Oxford University Press, 2004), pp. 159–69.

Oppel, John, 'Saint Jerome and the History of Sex', *Viator*, 24 (1993), 1–22.

Bibliography

Paris, John Ayrton, *Medical Jurisprudence, by J. A. Paris and J. S. M. Fonblanque*, 3 vols. (London: W. Phillips, 1823), MML.

Parla, Ayse, 'The "Honor" of the State: Virginity Examinations in Turkey', *Feminist Studies*, 27.1 (2001), 65–89.

Peek, Wendy Chapman, 'King by Day, Queen by Night: The Virgin Camille in the *Roman d'Eneas*', in *Menacing Virgins*, ed. Kelly and Leslie, pp. 71–82.

Pelham, R. W., 'A Shaker's Answer to the Oft-Repeated Question, "What Would Become of the World If All Should Become Shakers?"', in Avery, *Sketches*, pp. 31–46.

Petroff, Elizabeth Avilda, *Body and Soul: Essays on Medieval Women and Mysticism* (New York: Oxford University Press, 1994).

Phillips, Kim M., 'Four Virgins' Tales: Sex and Power in Medieval Law', *Medieval Virginities*, ed. Bernau, Evans and Salih, pp. 80–101.

— 'Written on the Body: Reading Rape from the Twelfth to the Fifteenth Centuries', in *Medieval Women and the Law*, ed. Noël James Menuge (2000; repr. Woodbridge: Boydell Press, 2001), pp. 125–44.

— *Medieval Maidens: Young Women and Gender in England, 1270–1540* (Manchester: Manchester University Press, 2003).

'Philogamus', from *The Present State of Matrimony; or, The Real Causes of Conjugal Infidelity and Unhappy Marriages* (1739), in *Women in the Eighteenth Century*, ed. Jones, pp. 77–81.

Pivar, David J., *Purity Crusade: Sexual Morality and Social Control 1868–1900*, Contributions in American History, 23 (Westport, CT: Greenwood Press, 1973).

Poos, L. R., 'Sex, Lies, and the Church Courts of Pre-Reformation England', *Journal of Interdiscplinary History*, 25. 4 (Spring 1995), 585–607.

Porter, Jane, *The Sheikh's Virgin* (Richmond: Harlequin Mills & Boon, 2005).

'Public Support for Comprehensive Sexuality Education. (SIECUS Fact Sheet)', *SIECUS Report*, 32.4 (Fall 2004), p. 39 (3).

Raknem, Ingvald, *Joan of Arc in History, Legend and Literature* (Oslo, Bergen, Tromsö: Universitetsforlaget, 1971).

Ralegh, Sir Walter, *The Discoverie of the Large, Rich and Bewtiful Empire of Guiana* (London: Robert Robinson, 1596), EEBO.

Rayner, Jay, 'Kiss Chaste', *Observer*, 11 September 2005, p. 20.

Revolve: The Complete New Testament (n.p.: Thomas Nelson, 2003).

Revolve2: The Complete New Testament (n.p.: Thomas Nelson, 2004).

Richards, Jeffrey, *Sex, Dissidence and Damnation: Minority Groups in the Middle Ages* (London: Routledge, 1990).

Riddy, Felicity, 'Temporary Virginity and the Everyday Body: *Le Bone Florence of Rome* and Bourgeois Self-making', in *Pulp Fictions of Medieval England: Essays in Popular Romance*, ed. Nicola McDonald (Manchester: Manchester University Press, 2004), pp. 197–216.

Roberts, Hannah, 'Reconstructing Virginity in Guatemala', *Lancet*, 367.9518 (15 April, 2006), pp. 1227–8, ScienceDirect.

Robertson, William George Aitchison, *Manuals of Medical Jurisprudence and Toxicology*, 4th edn (1908; London, 1921), MML.

Rogers, John, 'The Enclosure of Virginity: The Poetics of Sexual Abstinence in the English Revolution', in *Enclosure Acts: Sexuality, Property, and Culture in Early Modern England*, ed. Richard Burt and John Michael Archer (Ithaca: Cornell University Press, 1994), pp. 229–50.

Rostosky, Sharon Scales, Mark D. Regnerus and Margaret Laurie Comer Wright, 'Coital Debut: The Role of Religiosity and Sex Attitudes in the Add Health Survey', *Journal of Sex Research*, 40.4 (November 2003), 358 (10).

Russell, Sir William Oldnall, *A Treatise on Crimes and Misdemeanors*, 2 vols., 1st American edn, by Daniel Davis (Boston, 1824), MML.

Saunders, Corinne, *Rape and Ravishment in the Literature of Medieval England* (Cambridge: D. S. Brewer, 2001).

St Ambrose, 'Concerning Virgins', *Ambrose: Select Works and Letters*, in *Nicene and Post-Nicene Fathers*, ed. Philip Schaff, 2nd series, 14 vols. (1890–98; Peabody, MA: Hendrickson, 1994), X, p. 374, <http://www.ccel.org/ccel/schaff/npnf210.iv.vii.iii.ii.html>.

Sawyer, Miranda, '50,000 Rapes Each Year but Only 600 Rapists Sent to Jail', *Observer*, 31 July 2005, <http://observer.guardian. co.uk/uk_news/story/0,6903,1539646,00.html>.

Schibanoff, Susan, 'True Lies: Transvestism and Idolatry in the Trial of Joan of Arc', in *Fresh Verdicts on Joan of Arc*, ed. Bonnie Wheeler and Charles T. Wood (1996), pp. 31–60.

'Sex UK: The Facts', *Observer*, 22 January 2006, p. 17.

— William Shakespeare, *A Midsummer Night's Dream*, in *The Riverside Shakespeare*, pp. 217–49.

— *Henry VI, Part I*, in *The Riverside Shakespeare*, pp. 587–629.

— *The Tempest*, in *The Riverside Shakespeare*, pp. 1606–38.

— and John Fletcher, *Two Noble Kinsmen*, in *The Riverside Shakespeare*, pp. 1642–81.

Shalit, Wendy, *A Return to Modesty: Discovering the Lost Virtue* (New York, NY: Touchstone, 2000).

Bibliography

Sharp, Mrs Jane, *The Midwives Book; or, The Whole Art of Midwifry Discovered* (1671), EEBO.

Shinners, John, ed., *Medieval Popular Religion, 1000–1500: A Reader*, Readings in Medieval Civilizations, II (1997; Peterborough, Ontario: Broadview Press, 1999).

Shohet, Lauren, 'Figuring Chastity: Milton's Ludlow Masque', in *Menacing Virgins*, ed. Kelly and Leslie, pp. 146–64.

Smith, Christian, *Christian America? What Evangelicals Really Want* (Berkeley: University of California Press, 2000).

Smith, Kevin, *Chasing Amy*, in *'Clerks' and 'Chasing Amy': Two Screenplays by Kevin Smith* (New York: Miramax Books, 1997), pp. 173–301.

Sommers, Annie Leah, and Michael A. Sommers, *Everything You Need to Know About Virginity*, The Need to Know Library (New York: The Rosen Publishing Group, 2000).

Stephens, Carla, *A Passion for Purity: Protecting God's Precious Gift of Virginity* (Tulsa, OK: Harrison House, 2003).

Stephens, Susan, *Virgin for Sale* (Richmond: Mills & Boon, 2005).

Sturges, Robert S., 'The Pardoner, Veiled and Unveiled', in *Becoming Male in the Middle Ages*, ed. Jeffrey Jerome Cohen and Bonnie Wheeler (New York: Garland, 1997), pp. 261–77.

Sullivan, Karen, *The Interrogation of Joan of Arc*, Medieval Cultures, 20 (Minneapolis: University of Minnesota Press, 1999).

Tate, Nahum, 'The Virgin', from *A Present for the Ladies* (1693), LION.

Taylor, Andrew, 'Reading the Dirty Bits', in Jacqueline Murray and Konrad Eisenbichler, eds., *Desire and Discipline: Sex and Sexuality in the Premodern West* (Toronto: University of Toronto Press, 1996), pp. 280–95.

Taylor, Jeremy, *Holy Living*, ed. P. G. Stanwood (Oxford: Clarendon, 1989).

Tertullian, 'On the Veiling of Virgins', in *Ante-Nicene Fathers*, ed. Allan Menzies, 4th edn, 10 vols. (Peabody, MA: Hendrickson, 1994), IV, pp. 27–38.

The Awful Disclosures of Maria Monk (Bexhill-on-Sea: AKS Books, 2004).

The Life of Christina of Markyate: A Twelfth-Century Recluse, ed. and trans. C. H. Talbot (1959; Toronto: University of Toronto Press, 1998).

The N-Town Play, ed. Stephen Spector, 2 vols., Early English Text Society, supplementary series 11, 12 (Oxford: Oxford University Press, 1991).

The Travels of Sir John Mandeville, trans. C. W. R. D. Moseley (London: Penguin, 1983).

Thurian, Max, *Marriage and Celibacy*, trans. from the French, *Mariage et Célibat* (1955) by Norma Emerton, Studies in Ministry and Worship (London: SCM Press, 1959).

Tidy, Charles Meymott, *Legal Medicine*, 2 vols. (London: Smith, Elder, 1882–3), MML.

Underhill, Rosemary A., and John Dewhurst, 'The Doctor Cannot Always Tell: Medical Examination of the "Intact" Hymen', *Lancet*, 311.8060 (18 February 1978), pp. 375–6, ScienceDirect.

Venette, Nicolas, 'Chap. IV: If there be any Signs of a Maidenhead', in *Conjugal Love Reveal'd* (1687; first printed in English in 1703; London: 1720?, 7th edn), ECCO.

Villaruel, Antonia M., 'Cultural Influences on Sexual Attitudes, Beliefs, and Norms of Young Latina Adolescents', *Journal of the Society of Pediatric Nurses*, 3.2 (April/June 1998), 69 (11).

Vincent, Louise, 'Virginity Testing in South Africa: Re-Traditioning the Postcolony', *Culture, Health & Sexuality*, 8.1 (January/February 2006), 17–30.

Vives, Juan Luis, *A Very Fruitful and Pleasant Book Called the Instruction of a Christen Woman*, trans. by Richard Hyrde (London, 1529), EEBO.

'Virginity Pledges Do Not Predict Risk of Sexual Infections', *Nursing Standard*, 20.2 (September 2005), 19 (1).

Walker, Garthine, 'Rereading Rape and Sexual Violence in Early Modern England', *Gender and History*, 10.1 (April 1998), 1–25.

Wallis, Jim, *God's Politics: Why the American Right Gets It Wrong and the Left Doesn't Get It* (Oxford: Lion Hudson, 2005).

Walters, Joanna, 'No Sex is Safe Sex for Teens in America', *Observer*, 2 January 2005, p. 22.

Warner, Marina, *Alone of All Her Sex: The Myth and the Cult of the Virgin Mary* (London: Weidenfeld and Nicolson, 1976).

— *Joan of Arc: The Image of Female Heroism* (1981; Berkeley: University of California Press, 2000).

Waterworth, J., ed. and trans., *The Council of Trent: The Twenty-Fourth Session: The Canons and Decrees of the Sacred* (London: Dolman, 1848).

Weeks, Jeffrey, *Sex, Politics and Society: The Regulation of Sexuality Since 1800* (London and New York: Longman, 1981).

— *Sexuality and Its Discontents: Meanings, Myths and Modern Sexualities* (London: Routledge, 1985).

Weld, Elizabeth Catherine, 'Concerning the Proofs of Virginity', in *The Cases of Impotency and Virginity Fully Discuss'd* (London, 1732), pp. 43–62, ECCO.

Westphal, Sarah, 'Camilla: The Amazon Body in Medieval German Literature', *Exemplaria*, 8.1 (1996), 231–58.

Bibliography

Whytt, Robert, *Observations on the Nature, Causes, and Cure of Those Disorders Which Have Been Commonly Called Nervous, Hypochondriac, or Hysteric*, 3rd edn (Edinburgh, 1767), ECCO.

Wilkes, Wetenhall, 'A Letter of Genteel and Moral Advice to a Young Lady' (1740; 8th edn 1766), in *Women in the Eighteenth Century*, ed. Jones, pp. 29–35.

Wilson, Lee, 'Foreword', in Stephens, *A Passion for Purity*.

Winstanley, Gerrard, *Fire in the Bush* (London, 1650), pp. 50–51, EEBO.

Wogan-Browne, Jocelyn, 'Virginity Now and Then: A Response to Medieval Virginities', in *Medieval Virginities*, ed. Bernau, Evans and Salih, pp. 234–53.

Yates, Frances, *Astraea: The Imperial Theme in the Sixteenth Century* (London and Boston: Routledge and Kegan Paul, 1975).

Index

Numbers in *italics* refer to illustrations.

Index

Index

Index

transvestite virgins, 36
The Trial (play), 97, 99
Trust for the Study of Adolescence, 173

'Upon Appleton House' (Andrew Marvell), 112
urine: quality of as sign of virginity, 7
Ursula, St, *35*
uterus
    as crucial to health, 13, 16
    size of as sign of virginity, 7–8
    'vapours', 16

The V Club (Kate Brian), 95–7, 100, 108, 117
vaginal surgery, 26–9
'vapours', 13
'Venemous Virgin', 12
Venette, Nicolas, 32
viragints, 20, 21
'The Virgin' (Nahum Tate), 86, 89–90
Virgin for Sale (Susan Stephens), 87
'A Virgin Life' (Jane Barker), 107, 118
'The Virgin Martyr' (Ada Cambridge), 123
Virgin Mary, 34, 39, 46–9, 97, 99–100
virgin mummies, 29–30
The Virgin Suicides (Jeffrey Eugenides), 124–7
virgin territories, 134–6
The Virgin Unmask'd (Bernard Mandeville), 90–1
Virginia, 135
virginity
    and abstinence education, 171–85
    Catholic thought on, 31–45, 50
    and celibacy, 39–40
    and defloration, 102–6, 136
    in eighteenth-century literature, 83–5

evangelical attitudes to, 58–70
faking of, 9, 37
as freedom giving, 106–9, 150–3
Freud on, 24–5
as a gift, 117–18
as guaranteeing legitimacy of offspring, 33, 140–2
as harmful, 12, 13–20, 120–4
innocence vs nubility, 88–95
loss of, 37, 102–6, 124–7, 170, 183–4
and marriage, 40–3
in Medieval literature, 72, 74–6, 77, 87–8
in modern literature, 78–80, 81
persistence of ideal of, 25–6, 28
physical signs of, 1–10, 160–2
pledges, 181–2
Protestant thought on, 46, 49–50, 51, 52–70
and rape, 155–8, 161–3
'regaining' of, 26–9
and the religious life, 41–5
and reputation, 95–7, 99
in romance novels, 78–9, 86
of royalty, 131–4
'secondary', 69
in seventeenth-century poetry, 82–3
shame of losing, 138–40
testing of, 100–3
and truthfulness, 86–8
as unnatural, 118–19
voluntary, 20–1, 41–3
vulnerability arising from, 137
Virgins Complaint for the Loss of Their Sweethearts, 121–2
Vives, Juan, 138–40, 141–2
Votes and Wages (1912), *151*

Watton, Nun of, 37–9, 43, 137
Waxman, Henry A., 176, 178
Weeks, Jeffrey, 169